ANCIENT PRESCRIPTION FOR HEALTH

"This book was born as a result of a thousand sighs for the many people who left my office without receiving adequate help. I have written the prescription that I would have given these patients if only I had the time.

"I hasten to add that the counsel is not original with me. When God led the Israelites out of afflicted Egypt, He promised them that if they would obey His statutes, He would put *none of these diseases* upon them . . ."

—S. I. McMillen, M.D.

None
of
These
Diseases

S. I. McMillen, M.D.

Dedicated to
A MOTHER
A SISTER
A WIFE
A DAUGHTER

Copyright © 1963 by Fleming H. Revell
Published by Fleming H. Revell
a division of Baker Book House Company
P.O. Box 6287, Grand Rapids, MI 49516-6287

Library of Congress catalog card number: 63-13359
ISBN 0-8007-8030-2

October 1993

Printed in the United States of America

Scripture quotations identified KJV are from the King James Version of the Bible.

Scripture quotations identified as ASV are from the New American Standard Version of the Bible. Used by permission of Thomas Nelson, Inc., original publisher of the American Standard Version.

Scripture quotations identified as *Berkeley* are from the MODERN LANGUAGE BIBLE: THE BERKELEY VERSION IN MODERN ENGLISH. Copyright © 1945, 1959, 1969 by Zondervan Publishing House. Used by permission.

Scripture quotations identified as *Moffatt* are from *The Bible: A New Translation,* by James Moffatt, Copyright by James Moffatt, 1954. Used by permission of Harper & Row, Publishers, Incorporated.

Scripture quotations identified as *Phillips* are reprinted with permission of The Macmillan Company from *The New Testament in Modern English,* by J. B. Phillips, Copyright, 1958 by J. B. Phillips.

Scripture quotations identified as NEB are from *The New English Bible.* © The Delegates of the Oxford University Press and The Syndics of the Cambridge University Press 1961, 1970. Reprinted by permission.

PREFACE

Peace does not come in capsules! This is regrettable because medical science recognizes that emotions such as fear, sorrow, envy, resentment and hatred are responsible for the majority of our sicknesses. Estimates vary from 60 per cent to nearly 100 per cent.

Emotional stress can cause high blood pressure, toxic goiter, migraine headaches, arthritis, apoplexy, heart trouble, gastrointestinal ulcers, and other serious diseases too numerous to mention. As physicians we can prescribe medicine for the symptoms of these diseases, but we can not do much for the underlying cause—emotional turmoil. *It is lamentable that peace does not come in capsules.*

We need something more than a pill for the disease-producing stresses of the man who has lost his life's savings, the tearful feminine soul who has been jilted, the young father who has an inoperable cancer, the woman whose husband is a philanderer, the distraught teen-ager with a facial birthmark, and the schemer who lies awake at night trying to think of ways to get even with his neighbor.

This book was born as a result of a thousand sighs for the many people who left my office without receiving adequate help. There wasn't time to do much more than prescribe some pills for their complaints, but I knew there was something better than pills for them to take for the rest of their lives. In this book I have written the prescription I would have given to those patients if only I had had the time.

I hasten to add that this counsel is not original with me. When God led the Israelites out of afflicted Egypt, He promised them that if they would obey His statutes, He would put *"none of these diseases"* upon them. God guaranteed a freedom from disease that modern medicine cannot duplicate. Was the divine pledge a hollow assurance? Were the Israelites miraculously freed from these diseases? Would the same regulations save us today?

I am confident that the reader will be intrigued to discover that the Bible's directives can save him from certain infectious diseases, from many lethal cancers, and from a long gauntlet of psychosomatic diseases that are increasing in spite of all efforts of modern medicine.

Debts of gratitude are due many people. First, I owe much to my patients. Although many case histories are given, they are carefully disguised with fictitious names and altered circumstances, and are combined with the histories of other patients.

This book could never have been born without the sympathetic help of Dr. Gustav Prinsell and Dr. J. Myron Stern who took excellent care of my practice for nearly nine months. Another kind of doctor, Ray W. Hazlett, Litt. D., gave me encouragement and help in the first months when I could have given it up so easily.

I am most grateful to Miss Sophie Davis who washed away all the grammatical errors and rubbed it with plenty of commas and marks like that. To Mrs. Muriel Babbitt goes the credit of dressing and redressing the little offspring with neatly typewritten sheets, so that it might look its best for the publisher.

My daughter Linda and her husband, Dr. J. Myron Stern, gave me quite a few stinging "vitamin shots" for which I am now grateful. To Alice Jean, my wife, goes my deepest appreciation for her constant support and encouragement.

Above all, I thank the Lord for His gracious guidance and help manifested to me in many ways.

CONTENTS

CHAPTER 1

Gray Hair and Rattlesnake Oil

"TO PREVENT THE HAIR FROM TURNING GRAY, ANOINT IT with the blood of a black calf which has been boiled in oil, or with the fat of a rattlesnake."[1] This prescription comes from the famous *Papyrus Ebers,* a medical book written in Egypt about 1552 B.C. Since Egypt occupied the dominant position in the ancient medical world, the *Papyrus* is of great importance as a record of the medical knowledge of that day.

The book also contains prescriptions for people who are losing hair: "When it falls out, one remedy is to apply a mixture of six fats, namely those of the horse, the hippopotamus, the crocodile, the cat, the snake, and the ibex. To strengthen it, anoint with the tooth of a donkey crushed in honey."[2] An extra-special hair dressing for the Egyptian Queen Schesch consisted of equal parts of a heel of an Abyssinian greyhound, date blossoms, and asses' hoofs, boiled in oil. The choice preparation was intended to make the royal hair grow.

To save victims bitten by poisonous snakes, physicians of that day gave them "magic water" to drink—water that had been poured over a special idol.[3] To embedded splinters they applied worms' blood and asses' dung. Since dung is loaded with tetanus spores, it is little wonder that lockjaw took a heavy toll of splinter cases.

Several hundred remedies for diseases are advised in the *Papyrus Ebers.* The drugs include "lizards' blood, swines' teeth, putrid meat, stinking fat, moisture from pigs' ears, milk goose grease, asses' hoofs, animal fats from various sources, excreta from animals, including human beings, donkeys, antelopes, dogs, cats, and even flies."[4]

About the time this Egyptian medical book was written, Moses was born in Egypt. Although his parents were

Israelites, he was raised in the royal court and "was learned in all the wisdom of the Egyptians. . . ."[5] There is little doubt that he was well acquainted with the medical knowledge of his time. Many thousands of the Israelites also knew and no doubt had used some of the common remedies mentioned in the *Papyrus Ebers.*

However, when Moses led the great company of Israelites out of Egypt, the Lord gave him a most remarkable promise for the new nation: "If thou wilt diligently hearken to the voice of the Lord thy God, and wilt do that which is right in his sight, and wilt give ear to his commandments, and keep all his statutes, *I will put none of these diseases upon thee,* which I have brought upon the Egyptians: for I am the Lord that healeth thee."[6]

". . . *none of these diseases* . . ."! What a promise! Had not the Egyptians and Israelites been afflicted with these diseases for ages? The remedies in their medical books had accomplished practically nothing; often they were worse than the diseases. Yet here was the Lord making a fantastic promise to free the Israelites of all the Egyptian diseases.

God proceeded to give Moses a number of commandments, which form part of our Bible today. Because these divinely given medical directions were altogether different from those in the *Papyrus Ebers,* God surely was not copying from the medical authorities of the day. Would Moses, trained in the royal postgraduate universities, have enough faith to accept the divine innovations without adding some of the things he had been taught? From the record we discover that Moses had so much faith in God's regulations that he did not incorporate a single current medical misconception into the inspired instructions. If Moses had yielded to a natural inclination to add even a little of his modern university training, we would be reading such prescriptions as "the heel of an Abyssinian greyhound," or "the tooth of a donkey crushed in honey," not to mention the drugs the leading physicians were compounding out of the bacteria-laden dung of dogs, cats and flies.

The divine instructions were not only devoid of harmful practices, but had many detailed positive recommendations. Let us take a glance at the impact of those positive instructions on the history of prevention of infectious diseases.

For many hundreds of years the dreaded disease leprosy had killed countless millions of people in Europe. The extent of the horrible malady among Europeans is given by Dr. George Rosen, Columbia University professor of public health: "Leprosy cast the greatest blight that threw its shadow over the daily life of medieval humanity. Fear of all other diseases taken together can hardly be compared to the terror spread by leprosy. Not even the Black Death in the fourteenth century or the appearance of syphilis toward the end of the fifteenth century produced a similar state of fright. . . . Early in the Middle Ages, during the sixth and seventh centuries, it began to spread more widely in Europe and became a serious social and health problem. It was endemic particularly among the poor and reached a terrifying peak in the thirteenth and fourteenth centuries."[7]

What did the physicians offer to stop the ever-increasing ravages of leprosy? Some taught that it was "brought on by eating hot food, pepper, garlic and the meat of diseased hogs." Other physicians said it was caused by malign conjunction of the planets. Naturally, their suggestions for prevention were utterly worthless.

Another plague that made the Dark Ages really dark was the Black Death. In the fourteenth century alone, this killer took the lives of one out of four persons, an estimated total of sixty million. It was the greatest disaster ever recorded in human history: "Sweeping everything before it, this plague brought panic and confusion in its train. . . . The dead were hurled pell-mell into huge pits, hastily dug for the purpose, and putrefying bodies lay about everywhere in the houses and streets. The sexton and the physician were cast into the same deep and wide grave; the testator and his heirs and executors were hurled from the same cart into the same hole together."[8]

What brought the major plagues of the Dark Ages under control? George Rosen gives us the answer:

Leadership was taken by the church, as the physicians had nothing to offer. The church took as its guiding principle the concept of contagion as embodied in the Old Testament. . . . This idea and its practical consequences are defined with great clarity in the book of Leviticus. . . . Once the condition of leprosy had been established, the patient was to be segregated and excluded from the community.

Following the precepts laid down in Leviticus the church undertook the task of combatting leprosy . . . it accomplished the first great feat . . . in methodical eradication of disease.[9]

The procedures came from Leviticus 13:46: "All the days wherein the plague shall be in him he shall be defiled; he is unclean: he shall dwell alone; without the camp shall his habitation be." Other historians credit the Bible for the dawning of a new era in the effective control of disease: "The laws against leprosy in Leviticus 13 may be regarded as the first model of a sanitary legislation."[10]

As soon as the European nations saw that the application of Scriptural quarantine brought leprosy under control, they applied the same principle against the Black Death. The results were equally spectacular, and millions of lives were saved.

If the lethal plagues had continued unabated, many celebrities of the Renaissance might never have been born, or they might have died untimely deaths. Thus, European history was greatly influenced because men began to practice the words of God to the Israelites: "If thou wilt diligently hearken to the voice of the Lord thy God, . . . I will put none of these diseases upon thee. . . ."

CHAPTER 2

Pride and Prejudice Versus Proof

ALTHOUGH EUROPE BROUGHT ITS MOST DEVASTING PLAGUES under control by obeying the Biblical injunction to isolate the victims, other important diseases continued to decimate mankind because people did not take seriously God's promise that they would be freed from *all* diseases by their obedience to *all* the divine regulations. Hence, intestinal diseases such as cholera, dysentery, and typhoid fever continued to take a heavy toll of lives. Up to the close of the eighteenth century, hygienic provisions, even in the great capitals, were quite primitive. It was the rule for excrement to be dumped into the streets which were unpaved and filthy. Powerful stenches gripped villages and cities. It was a heyday for flies as they bred in the filth and spread intestinal diseases that killed millions.

Such waste of human lives that could have been saved if people had only taken seriously God's provision for freeing man of diseases! With one sentence the Book of books pointed the way to deliverance from the deadly epidemics of typhoid, cholera and dysentery: "You shall set off a place outside the camp and, when you go out to use it, you must carry a spade among your gear and dig a hole, have easement, and turn to cover the excrement."[1]

A medical historian writes that this directive is "certainly a primitive measure, *but an effective one, which indicates advanced ideas of sanitation.*"[2] How could this recommendation, which was given to Moses, possibly offer ideas of sanitation advanced 3,500 years ahead of him? The most logical explanation is that the Bible is what it claims to be: *the inspired Word of God.*

But the pride and prejudices of man are foes too strong for proof. Let me give an example by citing what happened in Vienna in the 1840's, when the Viennese were feasting on the superb waltzes of Johann Strauss and his son.

Vienna was also famous as a medical center. Let us look in on one of the famous teaching hospitals of that day, Allegemeine Krakenhaus. In the maternity wards of this celebrated hospital, one out of every six women died, and this frightening mortality rate was similar in other hospitals around the world. The obstetricians ascribed the deaths to constipation, delayed lactation, fear, and poisonous air.

When the women died, they were wheeled into the autopsy room. The first order of each morning was the entrance of the physicians and medical students into the morgue to perform autopsies on the unfortunate victims who had died during the preceding twenty-four hours. Afterward, without cleansing their hands, the doctors with their retinue of students marched into the maternity wards to make pelvic examinations on the living women. Of course, no rubber gloves were worn.

In the early 1840's, a little over a hundred years ago, a young doctor named Ignaz Semmelweis was given charge over one of the obstetrical wards. He observed that it was particularly the women who were examined by the teachers and students who became sick and died. After watching this heartbreaking situation for three years, he established a rule that, in his ward, every physician and medical student who had participated in the autopsies of the dead must carefully wash his hands before examining the living maternity patients.

In April, 1847, before the new rule went into effect, fifty-seven women had died in Dr. Semmelweis' ward. Then the rule of washing the hands was instituted. In June, only one out of every forty-two women died; in July, only one out of every eighty-four. The statistics strongly indicated that fatal infections had been carried from corpses to living patients.

One day, after performing autopsies and washing their hands, the physicians and students entered the maternity ward and examined a row of beds containing twelve women. Eleven of the twelve women quickly developed temperatures and died.

Another new thought was born in Semmelweis' alert brain: some mysterious element was evidently carried from one living patient to others, and with fatal consequences. Logically, Semmelweis ordered that everybody should wash his hands carefully after examining each living patient. Immediately howls of protest were raised against the "nuisance" of washing, washing, washing—but the mortality rate went further down.

Was Semmelweis acclaimed by his fellows? On the contrary, lazy students, prejudiced obstetricians, and jealous superiors scorned and belittled him so much that his annual contract was not renewed. His successor threw out the wash basins and up shot the mortality rate to the old terrifying figures. Were his colleagues convinced then? Not at all! We mortals might as well face it—the human mind is so warped by pride and prejudice that proof can rarely penetrate it.

For eight months Semmelweis tried to get a respectable position in the hospital again, but to no avail. Shocked and depressed, he left Vienna without saying good-by to his few friends and went to Budapest, his home city. There he obtained a position in a hospital; there too the mortality rate of pregnant women was frightful. Again he instituted the practice of washing the hands before examining the individual patient. At once the grim reaper was halted, but again prejudices and jealousies overpowered the proof and many of Semmelweis' colleagues passed him in the hospital corridors without speaking.

Dr. Semmelweis wrote an excellently documented book on his work, which only spurred his assailants to the bitterest sarcasm. The strain plus the death cries of dying mothers so haunted and weighed on his sensitive nature that his mind finally broke. Ignaz Semmelweis died in a mental institution without ever receiving the recognition he richly deserved.

Many, many centuries before Semmelweis, God gave to Moses detailed instructions on the safest method of cleansing the hands after handling the dead or the infected living.[8] Semmelweis' method of cleansing went a long way in preventing many deaths, but it would not be accepted in any hospital today. In contrast, the Scriptural method specified not merely washing in a basin, but repeated washings in *running water,* with time intervals allowed for drying and exposure to sun to kill bacteria not washed off. Furthermore, the Scriptural method also required contacts to change to clothes that had been washed and dried. The Biblical technique was so different from and so much more effective than anything man ever devised that, again, it is logical to believe the regulations were given, as the Bible claims, from God to Moses.

The spirit of pride and prejudice regarding the washing of hands also existed in surgery. During most of the nineteenth century the preliminaries of major surgery were frightfully simple. The patient came into the operating room, took off his trousers and underwear, and crawled up on the operating table. The surgeon took off his coat, rolled up his shirt sleeves, took some instruments out of a bag or a cupboard, and started to operate. If the surgeon wished his students to examine something inside the opening, he would have them step forward and poke their germ-covered hands into a sterile abdomen.

Of course, the mortality from surgery was frightful. Dr. Roswell Park tells about his own experiences in his book on medical history: "When I began my work, in

1876, as a hospital *interne,* in one of the largest hospitals in this country, it happened that during my first winter's experience, with but one or two exceptions, every patient operated upon in that hospital, and that by men who were esteemed the peers of any one in their day, died of blood poisoning. . . ."[4]

Such mortality would not have occurred if surgeons had only followed the method God gave to Moses regarding the meticulous method of hand washing and changing of clothes after contact with infectious diseases.

Dr. Park states that in the two years following 1876, the antiseptic method of cleansing hands and instruments was introduced, and there was a spectacular drop in the mortality rate. The work of John Tyndall, Louis Pasteur, Robert Koch, and Sir Joseph Lister finally furnished visible proof that slowly dispelled pride and prejudice.

In the twentieth century no surgical procedure is performed without meticulous scrubbing of the hands. However, any failure to wash the hands carefully when treating medical cases has resulted in needless loss of lives. Staphylococcus infections have become disastrous epidemics in some hospital nurseries. In the summer of 1958 an epidemic of a staph infection, caused by improperly washed hands, spread through a large general hospital in the eastern United States. The various antibiotics were of little help, and before the infection was brought under control it snuffed out the lives of eighty-six men, women and children.

The New York State Department of Health became alarmed because these infections could be spread so quickly by a carrier who failed to wash his hands carefully. In 1960 the Department issued a book describing a method of washing the hands, and the procedures closely approximate the Scriptural method given in Numbers 19.

At long last, in the year 1960, man finally muddled through. He learned, after centuries and at a frightful cost, what God gave to Moses by *inspiration.*

CHAPTER 3

Science Arrives
—Four Thousand Years Late

"DOCTOR, YOU MUST TELL ME WHETHER I HAVE CANCER or not. I insist. What do the reports from the laboratory show? I must know!" Pretty, thirty-six-year-old Beth Howard sat on the edge of her seat. For over two weeks her doctor had been using delaying tactics in order to condition her somewhat for this moment.

When the truth was given, it crushed her. "But, doctor, you can't let me die! You must save me. I couldn't possibly leave Lorna and Jane now. They are only in their teens. They need me now more than ever. Then Phil and Dick—and Bill—"

Sobbing, she buried her face in the pillow. At such a time many a doctor wishes he had taken up ditchdigging for a living. All he can give are pain killers and tranquilizers. Because Beth's cancer was advanced it was only a question of months before she would die.

Beth had cancer of the cervix. In the year she died, thirteen thousand other funerals went down our American streets with victims of this particular cancer. Many of them were middle-aged women, the peak incidence being between the ages of thirty-one and fifty.[1] Cancer of the cervix is one of the most common cancers in women. It comprises twenty-five per cent of all cancers in women and eighty per cent of all their genital cancers. These statistics are even more pathetic because *the large majority of deaths could have been prevented by following an instruction that God gave to Abraham.*

The history of this recognition is intriguing. In the early 1900's Dr. Hiram N. Wineberg, while studying records of patients in New York's Mount Sinai Hospital, observed that Jewesses were comparatively free from this common cancer.[2] It was an astonishing finding! Here was a group who had suffered far less from the giant killer than had other women.

Following this lead, Dr. Ira I. Kaplan and his associates studied their records at New York's Bellevue Hospital and were also astonished by the scarcity of cervical cancer among Jewish women.[3] In 1949 gynecologists at the Mayo Clinic noted that in 568 consecutive cases of cervical cancer, not a single Jewess was among the victims. Seven per cent of the admissions at Mayo Clinic are Jewish, and one would expect seven per cent of 568, or forty Jewesses, to have had uterine cancer. Instead, *there was not a single case.*[4] In 1954, in a vast study of 86,214 women in Boston, it was observed that cancer of the cervix in non-Jewish women was eight and one half times more frequent than in Jewish women.[5]

Why are Jewish women comparatively free of cervical cancer? Medical researchers now agree *that this spectacular freedom results from the practice of circumcision in Jewish men—which God ordered Abraham to institute four thousand years ago.*

A number of recent studies have borne out the fact that freedom from cancer of the womb is not due to factors such as race or food or environment, but wholly to circumcision. Other convincing studies were made in India. Although the people there have similar racial backgrounds, eat the same types of food, and live in the same climate and environment, the population is divided into two religious groups. Those who worship Mohammed, also a descendant of Abraham, practice circumcision. Among that group there is a much lower incidence of cervical cancer than among other women of the same race who eat the same food and live in the same environment.[6]

An editorial in the *American Journal of Obstetrics and Gynecology,* notes that both Jewish women and Indian Moslem women have a low incidence of cervical cancer, and observes that these two otherwise dissimilar people, have only one pertinent common denominator in their backgrounds—circumcision of the males. The editorial further records that in the Fiji Islands the cervical cancer rate is definitely lower among those people who practice circumcision. The editorial concludes with the advice that all newborn males should be circumcised to prevent this cancer.[7]

Medical science recognizes the fact, but unfortunately the general public is still unaware of the value of circumcision. How can circumcision of the male prevent cancer in women? The human male is cursed with a superabundance of foreskin over the penis. Circumcision (circum, "around," and cision, "cutting") remedies the fault by removing the excess of foreskin. If the tight, unretractable foreskin is not removed, proper cleansing can not be readily performed. As a result many virulent bacteria, including the cancer-producing Smegma bacillus, can grow profusely. During sexual intercourse these bacteria are deposited on the cervix of the uterus, but if the mucous membrane of the cervix is intact, little harm results. However, if lacerations exist, as they frequently do after childbirth, these bacteria can cause considerable irritation. Since any part of the body which is subjected to irritation is susceptible to cancer, it is perfectly understandable why cervical cancer is likely to develop in women whose mates are not circumcised.

These bacteria not only produce cancer in women, but also irritate the male organ and may cause cancer of the penis. The extreme rarity of penile cancer in circumcised men is shown by the fact that in 1955 only the fourth case in medical history was reported.[8] Thus we can say that circumcision is an almost perfect prophylaxis against this deadly cancer. Prevention by circumcision is far more important than treatment, because once a diagnosis of cancer is made, surgical removal of the penis is mandatory.

After many laborious years of study, medical science has at last accepted the best method of preventing two deadly cancers in men and women. Medical science has at last arrived—four thousand years late. Science did not arrive because of any laboratory steam that had been generated; it was carried forward by a long train of statistics—statistics that existed only because down through the years many generations of Jews had been faithful to the command that God gave to their father Abraham.[9]

Some people doubt the miracles by which God protected the Israelites during the plagues of Egypt, and dried up the Red Sea for their escape from bondage. Yet these miracles are small indeed compared to the miraculous, God-given directions that have saved the Israelites and others from plagues, epidemics and cancer for many centuries.

There is one final but remarkably unique fact about the

matter of circumcision. In November, 1946, an article in the *Journal of the American Medical Association* listed the reasons why circumcision of the newborn male is advisable. Three months later a letter from another specialist appeared in the same journal. He agreed heartily with the writer of the article on the advantages of circumcision, but he criticised him for failing to mention the safest time to perform the operation.[10]

This is a point well taken. L. Emmett Holt and Rustin McIntosh report that a newborn infant has "peculiar susceptibility to bleeding between the second and fifth days of life. . . . Hemorrhages at this time, though often inconsequential, are sometimes extensive; they may produce serious damage to internal organs, especially to the brain, and cause death from shock and exsanguination."[11] It is felt that the tendency to hemorrhage is due to the fact that the important blood-clotting element, vitamin K, is not formed in the normal amount until the *fifth* to the *seventh* day of life. If vitamin K is not manufactured in the baby's intestinal tract until the *fifth* to the *seventh* day, it is clear that the first safe day to perform circumcision would be the *eighth* day, the very day that Jehovah commanded Abraham to circumcise Isaac.

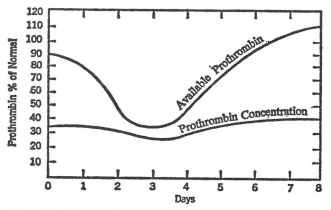

Composite Curves of Normal Infants Showing Concentration of Prothrombin and Available Prothrombin During First Week of Life, from Data of Owen, Hoffman, Ziffren and Smith.

A second element which is also necessary for the normal clotting of blood is prothrombin. A chart based on data discussed in *Holt Pediatrics* reveals that on the third day of a baby's life the available prothrombin is only thirty per cent of normal. Any surgical operation performed on a baby during that time would predispose to serious hemorrhage. From the chart we also see that the prothrombin skyrockets on the eighth day to a level even better than normal—110 per cent. It then levels off to 100 per cent. It appears that an eight-day-old baby has more available prothrombin than on any other day in its entire life. Thus

one observes that from a consideration of vitamin K and prothrombin determinations the perfect day to perform a circumcision is the *eighth* day.

We should commend the many hundreds of workers who labored at great expense over a number of years to discover that the safest day to perform circumcision is the eighth. Yet, as we congratulate medical science for this recent finding, we can almost hear the leaves of the Bible rustling. They would like to remind us that four thousand years ago, when God *initiated* circumcision with Abraham, He said, "And he that is eight days old shall be circumcised. . . ."[12]

Abraham did not pick the eighth day after many centuries of trial-and-error experiments. Neither he nor any of his company from the ancient city of Ur in the Chaldees had ever been circumcised. It was a day picked by the Creator of vitamin K.

The Old Testament circumcision was a symbol or type that looked forward to Christ and the circumcision He performs on the carnal heart:

In him also you were circumcised, not in a physical sense, but by being divested of the lower nature; this is Christ's way of circumcision.[13]

Then put to death those parts of you which belong to the earth—fornication, indecency, lust, foul cravings. . . . But now you yourselves must lay aside all anger, passion, malice. . . . now that you have discarded the old nature with its deeds. . . .[14]

As God required physical circumcision of the Jew, so today He requires of us "Christ's way of circumcision," which means "being divested of the lower nature" with its emotions of "anger, passion, malice" and self-centeredness. Such circumcision and such riddance of unlovely emotions are to man's great advantage, since *these emotions are clearly recognized by modern psychiatrists as causes or aggravations of the majority of all diseases.* Carnal emotions produce stress—which some authorities are now questioning as being the cause of all disease.[15]

While *physical* circumcision prevents two fatal cancers, Christ's *spiritual* circumcision of our evil nature prevents a far greater number of important diseases. Circumcision of the *body* looked forward to circumcision of the *spirit*.[16] Bodily circumcision is not required of Christians today because it looked forward to a greater circumcision that Christ now performs on the mind and heart of man.[17] Is it not intriguing and appropriate that both the *type* and the *fulfillment* prevent deadly diseases?

Failure of the Jew to observe the symbol of circumcision made him a spiritual outcast, and it is understandable why God makes Christ's circumcision a requirement of belonging to Him: "And those who belong to Christ Jesus have crucified the lower nature with its passions and desires."[18] Only when this divine surgery has been performed can man enjoy the promise of his heavenly Father—"none of these diseases."

CHAPTER 4

"Robber of Five Million Brains"

WHEN MY PHONE RANG ABOUT MIDNIGHT, I WAS VERY sleepy, but the voice on the other end aroused me instantly: "Say, Doc, can you come out here right away? Two people were killed on the highway, and two others are in desperate shape!"

A crowd was there when I arrived. The driver had hit a bridge abutment, and the steering wheel had flattened his chest. One look at him showed me that he was beyond human help. The other three occupants of the car had been hurtled twenty or thirty feet into a dry creek bed. One of them, a woman, was dead. A second woman was lying on the crumpled windshield that she took with her as she was propelled forward. She was moaning with pain. A semiconscious man was also down there in the mud and gravel of the creek.

What an unforgettable scene of devastation—the telescoped car, two mangled people covered with blood and mud, and two motionless figures who would never breathe again. The horror of the catastrophe was particularly pathetic because it could have been prevented. The brain of the driver had been robbed by a drug.

That ghastly night, I saw the destruction, suffering and death that can result when the brain of even one person is robbed. I confess that my mind is much too small to multiply the scenes of greater and lesser magnitude that occur daily because the brains of five million Americans are thus robbed.

Visualize another drunken driver as his school bus careens crazily over a steep, winding road. Imagine the havoc of twenty-six terrified, wide-eyed children, fearing for their lives, jumping out in ones and twos as the bus slows a bit on the curves.

In the *Journal of the American Medical Association,* Milton Golin summarizes his article, "Robber of Five Million Brains," with the statement: "Drink has taken five million men and women in the United States, taken them as a master takes slaves, and new acquisitions are going on at the rate of 200,000 a year."[1]

How many deaths are caused by partially decerebrated Americans on our highways? A study conducted in Delaware indicates that alcohol figures in about half of our traffic deaths.[2] In New York City a joint study made by the New York State Department of Health and Cornell University revealed that seventy-three per cent of the drivers responsible for the accidents in which they died had been drinking.[3] And in Westchester County, New York, blood tests were done on eighty-three drivers who were killed in single-vehicle accidents. The tests revealed that seventy-nine per cent of these drivers were "under the influence" of liquor.[4]

If one were to estimate that even fifty per cent of our

forty thousand annual automobile deaths were caused by John Barleycorn, it would mean a colossal indictment against the character of the annual mass murderer of twenty thousand American men, women and children. Many a driver has had his license taken away for causing one wanton death on the highway, yet here is one who is *legally* licensed to perpetuate the slaughter of thousands. He is indeed highly privileged to continue with such carnage.

In defense of this massacre, it is argued that our income taxes would be higher if the liquor industry did not exist. However, many studies indicate that a half dozen other costs would be lower. An insurance executive revealed that auto insurance rates could be cut forty per cent "if drinking drivers were not such a problem."[5]

What part do these five million Americans play in other types of violent deaths, such as homocide? I shall never forget the night I entered a house to find a drunken man pressing a cocked revolver against the temple of his wife, the mother of his five children. It was fortunate that I arrived when I did. Perhaps it was my presence that made him release her, but as he did, he said, "If I didn't think I would hang for this, I would blow your brains out."

A statistical study reveals that alcohol plays a prominent part in all kinds of violent deaths: "A résumé of 27 years of autopsy findings in Middlesex County, N.J., showed alcohol was a factor in 41.2 per cent of violent deaths, according to a report by the Chief Medical Examiner of the county, Dr. William C. Wilentz."[6] No drug known to man is more widely used nor more frequently responsible for deaths, injuries, or crimes than is ethyl alcohol.

Also revealing is a quick look at the matter of suicides, the eleventh leading cause of violent death, with an annual total close to twenty thousand. Expert statisticians estimate that alcohol is responsible for five thousand of these deaths.[7]

Alcohol robs brains in a variety of ways. When I was an intern, it was not uncommon to see a man ride into the hospital ward on a pink elephant. At least he thought he was riding one. If it wasn't a pink elephant, the man would be screaming because he was being charged by a herd of orange-colored buffaloes, or clawed by scarlet gorillas.

The large wards of that day became a bedlam as the

man shouted and sought refuge from the ferocious "animals" bent on his destruction. Sometimes he would try to escape from them by breaking a window to make a leap from the top floor. Fortunately the nurses were usually quick enough to grasp the tail of his nightgown and pull him back.

When we had to handcuff these patients to the beds and give them large doses of morphine, some of them died. Even today, under improved techniques, the mortality from delirium tremens is four per cent.[8]

Death results from other forms of alcoholic damage to the brain. Some victims develop disturbances of hearing, which can cause so much fear that they may commit suicide.

Alcohol is one of the most important factors in making mental disease the No. 1 health problem of America. A recent medical text states: "About 10% of the admissions to mental hospitals are officially reported as due to alcoholism, and another 10% have alcoholism of considerable degree noted as an important contributing cause. In addition, general hospitals take care of many of the acutely disturbed alcoholics."[9] In fact, six per cent of chronic alcoholics develop insanity in some form.[10] Because alcohol produces areas of atrophy in the brain, a large percentage of drinkers are actually committing a slow suicide of their personalities.

Alcohol, the licensed robber, every year kills many tens of thousands on our highways; it incites people to murder, homocide and suicide; it places others behind bars as raving maniacs. An amazed Shakespeare in his day exclaimed, "O God! that men should put an enemy in their mouths to steal away their brains. . . ."[11]

Furthermore, the effects of alcohol are certainly not limited to the anatomy above the ears. A drinker who was in my office recently complained that he couldn't raise his hands high enough to shave his beard. Not only does one out of every five alcoholics develop partial paralysis of certain muscles, but many of them complain bitterly about painful neuritis.

Hardening of the liver is a more serious affair because the blood from the gastrointestinal tract is prevented from flowing freely through the hardened liver. As a result of the back pressure in the veins, the lower extremities become badly swollen and the abdominal cavity is so distended with fluid that the victim can scarcely breathe. We can relieve the acute distress of the huge abdomen by inserting a hollow tube through the abdominal wall and drawing off some of the fluid, but unfortunately the fluid builds up in shorter intervals until the patient succumbs. The obstructed liver also can cause back pressure and ballooning of the veins of the esophagus. These thinned-out veins are prone to rupture when food is swallowed and can cause serious or fatal hemorrhage.

Hardening of the liver commonly occurs between the ages of thirty-five and sixty-five. When a physician witnesses the suffering and of men dying at a comparatively young age, he can not help but think of the way life is wasted in pursuit of its so-called pleasures.

I recall a certain New Year's Day. My wife and I arose refreshed and happy, and we thoroughly enjoyed a breakfast of grapefruit, cereal, ham and eggs. At noon we enjoyed to the full a New Year's dinner with all the luscious trimmings. But not so the other two couples who visited us. They had seen the New Year in with drinks and had spent the entire morning holding their heads, swallowing aspirin, and fighting severe nausea. None of the four could eat a bite of the superb feast. My wife and I discovered that life was much more wonderful without certain "pleasures!"

Alcoholics are deprived of the superlatives in life. Enjoyment is blurred or absent in areas of real living, such as recreation, music, art, eating, sex, sight and conversation. Some people hesitate to walk the Christian way because they do not want to give up certain "pleasures." These people need to embrace the promise: ". . . no good thing will he withhold from them that walk uprightly."[12] They need to understand that Biblical regulations have been written so that man might obtain the greatest amount of joy in life.

Food not only ceases to give enjoyment to the alcoholic, but often gives him great discomfort because of a severe inflammation of the lining of his stomach. He may be in torment from an ulcer, or lose many years from his life because of a resulting gastric cancer.

Alcohol not only robs a man of his brains and his health, but it robs his pocketbook. Money that should provide food, clothes, and proper housing for a man and family is far too often tossed over the bar. Many families never know anything of the niceties of living, and frequently their deprivations result in sickness and serious neglect.

The drinker also loses by the days he is not able to work. Statistics show that he loses a month's work every year. Yale University professors have also shown that his efficiency on the job is only fifty per cent.[13] Hence, they aptly refer to the drinker as the "half man," because he lacks discrimination and skill. He is likely to become involved in minor and major disputes with his fellows. His mind has been compared to a man driving a car in a fog, and in the factory he is accident-prone. A study of 340 patients who sustained accidental injuries revealed that forty-eight per cent had a blood level of over 0.5 gm. per liter.[14]

The revenues received from taxing the liquor industry fall far short of paying John Barleycorn's extravagant expenditures. A study made in France is most revealing: "In 1950 the direct cost of alcoholism to the country was about 132 billion francs, while the treasury revenues from alcoholic beverages was only 53 billion francs. There was therefore a loss to the country of nearly 80 billion francs. The loss of productivity caused by alcohol is estimated at about 325 billion francs a year.[15]

A publication of the American Medical Association reports that because of the industrial losses caused by this "half man" in industry, you and I are annually defrauded out of ten billion dollars.[16]

To these billions add the many more millions it costs to take care of the destitute families of alcoholics, to pay the bills of impoverished drinkers in their old age, and to pay for the institutional care of liquor's insane. A fraction of these billions of dollars would do much for medical research and would save mankind from a wide variety of ills.

This colossal waste of life and money is preventable by obedience to the Book of books, and "none of these diseases" is the promise to those who heed the many Scriptural injunctions against drunkenness. Here is one passage that warns in crisp but colorful language of the economic, medical and social aspects of drink, even including a description of delerium tremens:

Listen, my son, and be wise,
   be guided by good sense:
   never sit down with tipsy men or among gluttons;
   the drunkard and the glutton come to poverty,
   and revelling leaves men in rags. . . .
Who shriek? who groan?
Who quarrel and grumble?
Who are bruised for nothing?
Who have bleary eyes?
Those who linger over the bottle,
   those who relish blended wines.
Then look not on the wine so red,
   that sparkles in the cup;
   it glides down smoothly at the first,
   but in the end it bites like any snake,
   it stings you like an adder.
You will be seeing odd things,
   you will be saying queer things;
   you will be like a man asleep at sea,
   asleep in the midst of a storm.[17]

CHAPTER 5

Coronary and Cancer
By the Carton

THE MANAGER OF A GROCERY STORE PHONED ME ONE DAY.
"Doctor," he said, "I received a note from Mrs. Henderson,
which she smuggled out of her house. Her husband is
very sick, so sick that he is almost out of his head. He
won't allow her to leave the house for fear she will never
come back. She is afraid he may kill her. She wants you
to go to her house to examine her husband."

Mrs. Henderson's husband was over six feet tall. He
had been a strong muscular fellow, but now, his flesh
wasted away and his eyes sunk deep in their sockets, he
appeared more like a ghost than a man. For months he

hadn't slept well because he was coughing up masses of blood. His suffering and misery had been long and horrible. His wife was distracted and afraid of him because he had threatened to kill her if she attempted to leave him.

After I questioned and examined him, a diagnosis of cancer of the lung seemed highly probable. I made application by phone to have him admitted to the hospital and it was a big relief to all concerned when the day of his admission arrived. However, during his first night in the hospital, he had a severe hemorrhage and drowned in his own blood. An autopsy revealed widespread cancer of both lungs.

How often does this sanguinary horror occur in the lives of men and women? Every year thirty-five thousand Americans are strangled to death by lung cancer. This figure proclaims that no cancer statistic ever skyrocketed as high or as rapidly as lung cancer.

Back in 1912, lung cancer was, called "the rarest of diseases."[1] Then, in the 1920's, it began to increase. In the 1940's and 1950's, the mortality figures zoomed upward at an unbelievable rate.

In England, between 1924 and 1951, the death rates shot up tenfold while in Holland they soared twentyfold.[2] In New York State, in 1947, the death rate was frightening; yet even that high figure was doubled in 1957.[3] In the country as a whole during the past twenty years the death toll from lung cancer increased five hundred per cent.[4] At the present time more men die from it than from any other cancer; in fact, one out of every seven people who die of cancer has undergone the horrors of lung cancer. Authorities declare that soon every third person who dies of cancer will die of cancer of the lung. That is a far cry from 1912 when it was "the rarest of diseases."

What is the cause of lung cancer? When the statistics shot skyward, surgeons suspected the cause, but it was as late as 1949 that Dr. E. L. Wynder supplied the first statistical evidence of the relationship between smoking and lung cancer. In 1950 Wynder and Graham reported 684 proven cases of lung cancer in men and women. They discovered that of the 605 cases in men *only eight had been nonsmokers.*[5]

From England came a report from a study of 1,357

cases of lung cancer. In this vast group of victims, only seven nonsmokers were found.[6]

By 1958 eighteen scientific studies in five different countries proved that tobacco is undoubtedly the culprit committing yearly mass murder by strangling tens of thousands with the two ugliest words in medicine—lung cancer.[7]

The largest of the eighteen studies into the effects of smoking was made by the American Cancer Society.[8] This organization did follow-up studies on over 187,000 men, aged fifty to sixty-nine years, for a period of forty-four months. These men, comprising both smokers and nonsmokers, were typical Americans living in widely separated segments of the country. First, a careful questionnaire was made of the smoking habits of those who smoked. During these forty-four months, 11,870 men died. Photostatic copies of their death certificates were made and the causes of death were carefully tabulated.

The summary of this vast study not only proved beyond any doubt that smoking is the main cause of cancer of the lung, but it also revealed that smoking is responsible for *many other cancers of the body* and also a surprisingly large number of deaths from other diseases. The study revealed that in smokers there was:

1) an extremely high association for . . . cancer of the lung, cancer of the larynx, cancer of the esophagus, and gastric ulcers
2) a very high association for . . . pneumonia, and influenza, duodenal ulcer, aortic aneurysm, and cancer of the bladder
3) a high association for . . . coronary artery disease, cirrhosis hardening of the liver, and cancer of other sites
4) a moderate association for cerebral vascular lesions, strokes.[9]

While thirty-five thousand men and women currently die from cancer of the lung, smoking is also slaughtering even more from cancer in other sites. The surest way to die a painful and premature death is to buy cancer by the carton.

One wonders how smoking can produce cancer in organs such as the urinary bladder, which is far removed from the cigarette. But scientists have now identified in tobacco smoke eight different chemicals that can cause cancer when injected into animals. They are soluble products that can be spread throughout the body by the blood stream. One of these is 3-, 4-, 9-, 10-dibenspyrene. When it was injected into four thousand mice, every one of them developed cancer and died.[10]

Can filters eliminate these carcinogenics? Are filters a help or a hoax? Filters have been examined in elaborate studies which are summarized by the Surgeon General of the United States Public Health Service: "No method of treating tobacco by filtering the smoke has been demonstrated to be effective in materially reducing or eliminating the hazard of lung cancer."[11]

A few years ago I was called out of bed to treat a man who was experiencing severe pain over his heart. When I arrived, the man's face was ashen gray. His eyes were open, the pupils greatly enlarged, and his eyeballs insensitive to touch. He was not breathing; his heart was not beating. He had died of a heart attack caused by a large clot of the arteries, which supply the heart with its blood. The blocked coronary is the master of all executioners. He squeezed the life out of 474,000 men and women in this country in 1959.[12]

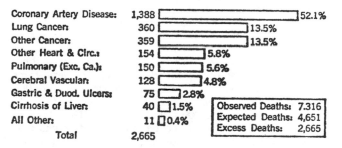

Coronary Artery Disease:	1,388	52.1%
Lung Cancer:	360	13.5%
Other Cancer:	359	13.5%
Other Heart & Circ.:	154	5.8%
Pulmonary (Exc. Ca.):	150	5.6%
Cerebral Vascular:	128	4.8%
Gastric & Duod. Ulcers:	75	2.8%
Cirrhosis of Liver:	40	1.5%
All Other:	11	0.4%
Total	2,665	

Observed Deaths: 7,316
Expected Deaths: 4,651
Excess Deaths: 2,665

Excess deaths among men with a history of
regular cigarette smoking

In my patient's shirt pocket was a partly empty pack of cigarettes. Can smoking cause heart disease? In the American Cancer Society's monumental study of 187,000 men, it was discovered that death from coronary artery disease was seventy per cent higher among smokers than among the comparable group of nonsmokers. This study revealed that the more a man smoked the greater was his liability of dying of heart disease. For those who smoked one half to one pack a day, the death rate was nearly double. For those who smoked two packs, the mortality was even higher.

I would like to call attention to one of the graphs made from the mammoth study by the American Cancer Society and published in the *Journal of the American Medical Association*. During the period of study there were 7,316 deaths among the group who smoked cigarettes. Statisticians figured that only 4,651 deaths would have occurred "if the age-specific death rates of the smokers had been the same as for men who never smoked." Subtracting the latter figure from the total, we see that 2,665 of *these deaths would not have occurred if the victims had not smoked*. [18] *In other words one out of every three of the men studied died because he was a smoker*. How many people would engage passage with an airline if the records showed that one out of every three passengers was doomed to die in a crash? *Yet one out of every three people who start off with cigarettes will experience a nicotine death*.

The metaphor of an airplane has another application. Once you commit yourself to a plane and take off, it is rather difficult to leave the plane, even if you decide you want to get out. Similarly, the individual who commits himself to smoking will soon be locked in by a habit from which he may not be able to escape.

What causes the death of such a huge percentage of smokers? In the graph one observes that *four times as many smokers die of coronary disease as die of lung cancer*. The study revealed that one out of every three coronary deaths is due to smoking. Since over 474,000 Americans died of bad coronaries, smoking is thus responsible for about 155,000 fatal heart cases. The appalling indictment of 70,000 cancer deaths against smoking is dwarfed by the fact that smoking kills 155,000 more with heart disease.

Not only is smoking the greatest single factor in causing lung cancer, but it is also the greatest factor in causing fatal heart attacks. Comparing a cigarette to a coffin nail is far more than a figure of speech.

By what mechanism does smoking cause a fatal heart attack? I recall the first time I saw the machine that measures the amount of blood flowing in the body. It was in 1956 at the Chicago meeting of the American

Medical Association. Doctors were asked to sit down and place one hand under the instrument. A basic reading was made on a revolving drum which recorded the amount of blood flowing in the arteries. After the basic reading was made, the physicians were given cigarettes to smoke. After only a few puffs on a cigarette, the recording needle on the revolving drum dropped rapidly, showing that smoking markedly reduces blood flow. Since coronary heart attacks are precipitated by a lack of blood in the coronary vessels, it is quite evident why smoking is responsible for many fatal heart attacks.

Another reason for these attacks is the fact that nicotine calls forth cholesterol which forms fatty tumors within the blood vessels, markedly reducing the flow of blood and facilitating clotting.

Reduction of blood flow and damage to the arteries can cause serious trouble in other organs. In the brain, the damaged arteries are prone to induce clots, the cause of strokes. A large-scale study revealed that the death rate from apoplexy is thirty per cent higher in smokers.[14] Since 192,980 people died from strokes of apoplexy in 1958,[15] the aforementioned percentage is decidedly startling.

As a result of the decreased blood flow, smokers are also likely to develop gangrene of the legs. After gangrene sets in, amputation of the leg is imperative.

Smoking can cause eye diseases and blindness.[16] It has also been indicted for its part in causing multiple sclerosis[17] and high blood pressure.[18] In pulmonary diseases, such as pneumonia, influenza, tuberculosis and asthma, the death rate is nearly three times as high as that of nonsmokers.[19]

Another common and serious condition caused by smoking is emphysema. This condition results from the "cigarette cough" that breaks down the delicate breathing cells of the lungs. Emphysema is even more common than cancer of the lung, with an outlook about as gloomy. A recent report of nineteen men and six women with this debilitating condition revealed that all of them had been heavy smokers.[20]

The danger of smoking to asthma cases is clearly enunciated in this quotation from the Mayo Clinic: "Smoking is one of the commonest sources of bronchial irritation, and invariably increases cough and asthma. Smoker's tongue, smoker's cough, smoker's throat, and smoker's bronchitis are no figments of the imagination, and when smoking is discontinued, these effects of tobacco smoking clear up in most instances. Smoking also has an irritating effect on the larynx. If a patient has asthma, he should not merely reduce smoking, he should completely stop it."[21]

Tobacco smoke can even affect others in the room. F. L. Rosen and A. Levy reported the case of an infant who had typical asthmatic attacks, which were promptly relieved when his parents stopped smoking and were reproduced when his parents resumed smoking.[22]

I was called out one evening to see a four-year-old boy fighting a life and death struggle to get his breath. He had been in a room in which half a dozen people were smoking. Even after he was taken to his bedroom, and in spite of adrenalin injections and other measures, his difficulty remained and he had to be moved out of the house to a smoke-free hospital room.

Ulcers of the gastrointestinal tract are also caused and aggravated by smoking. Every physician in general practice has a number of patients who are tortured by ulcers and who know that smoking is at the bottom of their trouble. In spite of their misery and the expenditure of hundreds of dollars for treatment, these people often curse heartily the day they began smoking but claim they can not stop it now.

Even duodenal ulcers, which are found beyond the stomach, cause twice as many deaths in smokers as compared to nonsmokers.[28] In the previously mentioned study by the American Cancer Society, there were fifty-one deaths from gastric ulcers. *Every one* of these deaths occured in a smoker.[24] In 1958 10,740 Americans died from duodenal and gastric ulcers. Smoking causes mass murder by the thousands in areas never suspected by the average citizen.

Mention should be made of the effect of smoking on women. The only reason that fewer women are suffering medical tragedies today is that they have not been smoking for as many years as men. Dr. P. Bernhard made studies on 5,458 women. If anything, tobacco has a more widespread effect on women than on men. For instance, he observed that disorders of the thyroid gland were nearly seven times more frequent among women who smoked than among women who did not. Menstrual disturbances were present in over thirty-six per cent of the smokers as compared to thirteen per cent of the nonsmokers. Symptoms of premature aging were observed in sixty-seven per cent of the smokers as compared to less than four per cent of the nonsmokers. Masculinization was more common among smokers. Also, there was an increase of miscarriages and premature births.[25]

If one were to total the deaths from cancer of the lung and other areas of the body, plus the deaths from apoplexy, pneumonia, influenza, tuberculosis, emphysema, asthma, ulcers and coronary heart trouble—deaths in which tobacco plays a major role—the grand total would be between two hundred thousand and three hundred thousand Americans per year.

Our U.S. Public Health Service has power to prevent this mass murder. Its power was demonstrated in October 1959, when the department put strict clamps on the sale of cranberries. There was only a remote chance that the spray used on the cranberries could have caused cancer in people, because a human being would have had to eat fifteen thousand pounds of cranberries to get the equivalent amount of spray used to induce cancer in mice. Because of the very possibility of such trouble, the government forbade the sale of sprayed cranberries—and just before our Thanksgiving dinners. But tobacco is a proven killer of tens of thousands each year and the government seems to close its eyes to the evidence.

Let us face squarely the reason behind this paradox. Any political party that attacked the five-billion-dollar tobacco industry would be committing political suicide. The cranberry companies could be squelched, but not the Goliaths of nicotine. Although the government counts its tobacco killings by the hundreds of thousands, it counts its profit from cigarette taxes by the hundreds of millions of dollars. Yet our government seems as devoid of conscience as an IBM machine. As Nero kept aloof and fiddled while Rome burned, so our government appears to be detached while the nicotine burning of over two hundred thousand American men and women occurs annually. We hope it may take action before tobacco claims multitudes more of American lives.

Why do people ever stick their heads into the noose of the smoking habit? Not because it is a pleasant sensation, since many are nauseated in the beginning. Why do they begin? I recall our arrival in Philadelphia from one of our African terms. While we were shopping in the large stores, our three-year-old daughter kept putting little pieces of paper between her lips and I kept pulling them out. Finally, I said, "Linda, why are you putting these pieces of paper between your lips?"

"Daddy, everybody in America has fire in their mouths. This is my fire."

To pre-teen-agers and teen-agers, smoking is the hallmark of maturity. It is an accreditation to show the world that they have arrived. Why do they continue? Nicotine, whether inhaled or injected with a needle, is a habit-producing drug that calls for more and more.

I remember a young woman who attended a nearby college a number of years ago. She thought it was sophisticated and smart to do a little smoking, under cover. She considered the college standards fanatical, radical and foolish. Because her style was cramped there, she finally went elsewhere.

Quite a few years have rolled by since then. To my surprise, she called me on the phone a few months ago to ask me what she could possibly do to stop smoking. Something had come up and she wanted to get rid of the habit. Was there any drug I could send her to deliver her from her bondage. Now she recognized that the maturity she was proud of a few years ago was actually a most disappointing immaturity. The freedom she sought had enslaved and tortured her.

One of my medical colleagues stopped smoking about six years ago, after having smoked most of his life. I asked him if he had found it difficult to stop. "No," he said, "not after I really made up my mind. When I quit, I got rid of the biggest nuisance in my life."

"What?" I retorted. "What do you mean? I thought people smoked because they derived fun from it."

He replied, "Not at all! I got rid of a grand nuisance. I was always looking for cigarettes, for matches, for places to put the ashes. I burned holes in my suits and the furniture. When I quit, I got rid of the worst nuisance anybody can ever have."

He is only one of many thousands of physicians who decided they were fools to continue smoking. A surprising change in attitude has occurred during the past eight years. The American Medical Association journals now will accept no advertising from cigarette companies, and no tobacco companies are allowed to take booths in AMA conventions.

Only a few years ago the air in our medical meetings was blue with smoke. For a day or two after attending the meetings I smelled like something smoked. In June 1961, in one of the section meetings held in New York City and attended by about two hundred physicians, I was so impressed by the nice clear air I was breathing that I decided to count how many doctors were smoking cigarettes. I only counted three, and a few years before I could have counted perhaps seventy-five. Some contrast!

A change in attitude has occurred because during recent years medical science has discovered and proved that smoking is the greatest single cause of:

> Public Killer No. 1—Heart disease
> Public Killer No. 2—Cancer.

Everybody should be thankful that medical science has its eyes open to the dangers of smoking. How much more thankful we should be to the Lord because He warned His people and saved countless thousands of His followers from a variety of horrible deaths many years before any scientific studies were done.

I recall the testimony of a man who was converted in an environment where there was no preaching against smoking. He stated that the Spirit of God told him to stop smoking. He said he thought it was very strange that God should make such an odd request of him, but he obeyed. Some time later he came across passages in the Bible that confirmed him in the course he had taken.

Although tobacco was not used when the Bible was written and is therefore not mentioned specifically, the impact of many verses has given sufficient warning to keep millions of Christians from using tobacco in any form. These admonitions, coupled with observations of tobacco users with their spittoons, smells, smoke, and sicknesses, have deterred the Christian from indulging. To a Christian, indulgence would be inconsistent with obedience to such Scriptures as:

What? know ye not that your body is the temple of the Holy Ghost which is in you ... and ye are not your own? For ye are bought with a price: therefore glorify God in your body, and in your spirit, which are God's.[26]

If any man defile the temple of God, him shall God destroy; for the temple of God is holy, which temple ye are.[27]

Whether therefore ye eat, or drink, or whatsoever ye do, do all to the glory of God.[28]

Obedience to God's Spirit and admonitions allows one to enjoy full-orbed living and His promise, "none of these diseases."

CHAPTER 6

They Have The Devil To Pay

CLICK-I-TY, CLICK, CLICK! IN AFRICA, WHEN WE HEARD THE rapid little clicks of a stick hitting the stony path, we knew it was Saturday, beggar's day. One of the first to arrive was blind Alpha, whose only eyes were on the end of his stick.

Who sinned?—this blind beggar or his parents? Probably his parents, since gonorrhea in the mother is the most common cause of lifelong blindness in the next generation. When the mother is infected with gonorrhea, the eyes of the baby can become infected as it passes through the birth canal. Gonorrheal infection of newborn babies is very severe and scars the eye so that the baby cannot see.

Africa and the East have their multiplied thousands of blind beggars, most of them blinded by gonorrhea. Their only food is the crumbs that seldom fall from the tables of an impoverished people. When they ask for bread, they often are pelted with stones, while a pack of lean, mangy dogs drive them out of town. When night comes, the beggars may carefully feel their way out of the forest to sleep on a porch, which affords some protection against torrential rains and wild jungle animals.

In our country we do not see blind beggars cluttering

our streets. Instead, they tap their way around the black corridors of our institutions. It wasn't many years ago that about ninety per cent of the blind in our institutions were there because of gonorrhea. Today, in countries where silver nitrate for the eyes of the newborn is not available, colossal indeed is the devastation to the eyes, bodies and lives from this venereal scourge. How tragic it is that hundreds of thousands of hopelessly blind people must pay the devil for the sins of their parents!

Syphilis is also the cause for many a baby born macer-ated and dead. If an infected baby lives, it may have various physical or mental deficiencies. Not only do these handicapped children have to pay a price during their lives, but their parents, as they look daily on their de-formed or insane children, must pay dearly and bitterly with lifelong remorse. In 1946 a medical text reported the state of affairs in the United States: "Each year it is estimated that . . . more than 50,000 infants with congenital syphilis are born."[1] No doubt penicillin has reduced this figure a great deal.

Some of these blighted children have offspring, who in their bodies and minds show sad evidences of the blasting character of syphilis. They exemplify the truth of the Scriptural warning of the visitation of "the iniquity of the fathers upon the children, and upon the children's chil-dren, unto the third and to the fourth generation."[2] In all, medical science recognizes five venereal diseases with their many scores of debilitating complications.

I shall not soon forget the first case of constriction of the urinary passage that I saw while I was in Africa. The victim was a man in his thirties. He gave a history of being unable to pass any urine from the normal passage for many years. The blocking of the passage was caused by an infection from "a lover." The urine thus obstructed had burrowed other little channels in his groin around the scrotum. He was indeed a pathetic character. He had found it was a costly business, this paying the devil.

Sometimes women have to pay a higher price than men. A few decades ago the opening statement from a professor of female diseases to his students was, "Curse the day when a woman walks into your office with a pelvic inflam-matory disease." He made this statement because of the frightful suffering and lifelong invalidism that gonorrhea can produce in women. The gonococcus, after providing a profusely purulent vaginitis, spreads upward through the womb to the tubes, ovaries, and the abdominal cavity. High fever, vomiting, and severe abdominal pain result, because of the localized peritonitis and abscess formation. After several weeks of such misery, a woman has respite for only a short time before recurrences of the same pain and symptoms. The chronic ill health, disability, suffering, sterility, unhappiness, and premature deaths caused by gonorrhea in backward areas of the world are still numbered in countless millions. These people have the devil to pay because they paid no attention to God's Word: "Neither let us commit fornication, as some of them committed, and fell in one day three and twenty thousand."[3]

With the advent of sulfa drugs and penicillin it was thought that venereal disease would be wiped out, because when penicillin was introduced in the early 1940's cases of venereal disease began to drop in civilized countries. This decrease continued until the 1950's when the trend started upward again in the United States.

Similarly, in Sweden there was a decrease in gonorrhea cases from 1946 to 1949. Now we read from there that gonorrhea has jumped "since 1949 by an extraordinary rise." In fact, between 1949 and 1952, gonorrhea actually "doubled in the county of Stockholm." By 1953 the number of gonorrheal cases reported exceeded the total of the ten other leading communicable diseases.[4] These increases occurred in spite of growing emphasis on educational propaganda. The devil surely collects his pay whenever and wherever people do not heed this Biblical warning: "Flee fornication. Every sin that a man doeth is without the body; but he that committeth fornication sinneth against his own body."[5]

American servicemen in Korea discovered that even penicillin did not prevent them from paying the devil. In 1959 Ernst Epstein reported that not only among our troops in Korea, but also among those in Japan, England, and America, studies indicated that strains of gonococcus were now becoming resistant to penicillin. He concludes: "From the clinical standpoint, the emergence of penicillin-resistant strains of N. gonorrhea has grave significance. No longer can acute gonorrhea be considered light-heartedly as a disease with a certain cure. . . . The twin problems of chronic gonorrhea in the male and the asymptomatic carrier . . . have returned. It is probably only a matter of time until penicillin resistance will be met on an increasing scale all over the world."[6] Further studies will be needed before we can accept this conclusion.

From England comes another report: "The fact that, in spite of penicillin and other antibiotics, venereal urethritis in men as well as gonorrhea in women has increased during 1952 should restrain any tendency to complacency about the venereal disease position, or any temptation to exaggerate the impact of antibiotics on these diseases. Sexual promiscuity is still rife and as long as this is the case, the danger of venereal disease remains."[7]

Young people and oldsters the world around are trying to avoid paying the devil, but medical statistics prove they are losing. Figures released from a national survey in 1957 show that "teenage venereal disease is increasing in 11 states; new epidemic outbreaks are reported in 19 states."[8] Comparing 1955 with 1959 figures for syphilis, we discover that in these four years the rate jumped: in Washington, D.C., 208%; Los Angeles, 291%; Houston, 378%; San Francisco, 591%; while New Orleans rates during this short period skyrocketed 818%.[9] The chief cause of the increase is attributable to a decline in moral standards.

There is a myth extant that venereal disease can be prevented if intelligence is used. A girl who had sexual relations with only one boyfriend thought she was safe. She was terribly shocked when her doctor told her she was infected. A "venereal tracer" revealed: the boy had consorted with only one other girl. This girl had had relations with five other men, who in turn had been with nineteen women, some of them prostitutes. The girl who thought her relationship had been limited to one person had had contact, through him, with at least ninety-two others.[10]

Legalized houses of prostitution, whose inmates are medically examined, do not prevent venereal disease, as was once thought. Actually, they increase the spread of these diseases. Dr. Walter Lentino, U.S. Army venereal disease control officer, asserts that in a study made, "80% of all cases of venereal disease came from houses of prostitution." These were all medically inspected houses. Dr. Lentino writes:

Medical inspection of prostitutes, even when performed with the utmost scrupulousness and honesty, cannot determine with even reasonable accuracy the infectivity of a prostitute. This being the case, any certification as to freedom from communicability of venereal disease in a prostitute is meaningless and gives a sanctified cloak to this business that is quite misleading. In fact, the unsuspecting tyro, who hears that the prostitutes are "medically O.K.'d" may require just this to remove the brakes of fear that may otherwise have stopped him from going to a house of prostitution and may, therefore, actually encourage venereal disease.[11]

Obedience to God's helpful Guidebook has been and still is the best way to avoid the calamitous effects of venereal disease. Everybody who stubbornly seeks to circumvent his heavenly Father's suggestions will sooner or later have to pay the devil's price.

The failure of penicillin is particularly conspicuous in its inability to treat some of the worst complications of syphilis. These sometimes develop before the individual is aware that he is infected. This is especially true of women, where the first ulcer of syphilis may be internal and pass unnoticed. The outstanding characteristic of syphilis is its tendency to awaken to destructive action many years after the original infection. Twenty or more years after the disease is contracted, it may strike down its victim with a dreaded or fatal complication.

One late manifestation of syphilis is paresis, an insanity caused by syphilis hitting the brain cells. This insanity can develop in a person from five to thirty years after the original infection. People between thirty-five and forty-five years of age are often affected. Little can be done unless treatment is instituted early. Unfortunately, early therapy is often delayed because the condition is similar to epilepsy, neurasthenia, or other insanities.

Another complication that may come on years after the initial infection is locomotor ataxia. Here the spinal nerves and occasionally the cranial nerves are involved. Disturbances of the cranial nerves may produce squints, blindness, or deafness. (Please do not diagnose everybody with squints, blindness, or deafness as having syphilis!) When the spinal cord is affected, the gait is characteristic—the foot is thrown out and then slapped down. Involvement of the bladder muscle can cause an inability to hold the urine.

In the light of the following description of locomotor

ataxia, one would do well to consider whether the illicit pleasure of a few seconds is worth lifelong misery:

At the time of sphincteric involvement, sexual debility and eventual impotence are almost invariable. . . . The most horrible of the tabetic symptoms are the crises which may be peripheral or visceral. Agonizing lightning pains occur in the muscles of the extremities, abdomen and chest. They are described by the patient as burning, gnawing, lancinating, twitching, or resembling a stabbing with a hot knife. The attacks come on with the rapidity of lightning; they may last for hours or days with brief intervals of freedom.[12]

Three thousand years ago our heavenly Father sought to save us from such an end:

My son, attend to wisdom,
    bend your ear to knowledge, . . .
    that they may save you from the loose woman:
    her lips drop honied words,
    her talk is smoother than oil itself,
    but the end with her is bitter as poison,
    sharp as a sword with double edge. . . .
Now listen to me, my son,
    hold fast to what I say:
    keep clear of her,
    never go near her door, lest . . .
    you are left at last to moan . . .
'Ah! why did I hate guidance,
why did I despise all warning?'[13]

The Lord not only gives many warnings to help mankind, but Jesus so transforms and fortifies one with the energy and power of His Holy Spirit that man has no valid excuse for falling into sexual sin. The Apostle Paul expresses the matter forcibly in his Epistle to the Thessalonians:

God's plan is to make you holy, and that entails first of all a clean cut with sexual immorality. Every one of you should learn to control his body, keeping it pure and treating it with respect, and never regarding it as an instrument for self-gratification, as do pagans with no knowledge of God. You cannot break this rule without in some way cheating your fellow-men. And you must remember that

God will punish all who do offend in this matter, and we have warned you how we have seen this work out in our experience of life. The calling of God is not to impurity but to the most thorough purity, and anyone who makes light of the matter is not making light of a man's ruling but of God's command. It is not for nothing that the Spirit God gives us is called the *Holy* Spirit.[14]

It must be bitter mockery, indeed, for people who steal a little illicit sexual pleasure to end with "sexual debility and eventual impotence." The type of sin often determines the pattern of the punishment.

Syphilis not only attacks the brain, causing insanity, and the spinal cord, causing the excruciating pains of locomotor ataxia, but it frequently attacks the heart. I remember a patient whose heart was devastated by syphilis. Though at first he denied any sexual safaris, he finally confessed that many years ago he was "kinda bad." And like Shylock of old, the devil wanted his "pound of flesh" right out of the heart. In fact, in the United States during 1945, the death rate from cardiovascular syphilis was reputedly the cause of forty thousand deaths.[15] The advent of penicillin reduced that figure, but we read that in 1953 "The management of cardiovascular syphilis . . . remains unsatisfactory, because the pathologic changes are the result of scarring."[16]

In spite of penicillin, in spite of venereal disease clinics, and in spite of educational programs, the U.S. Public Health Service reports that in 1957 there were one million fresh cases of gonorrhea. If we have these figures in the United States, highly favored with a host of antibiotics, it is staggering to the mind to imagine what the situation is among the great bulk of the world's population, many of whom are deprived of medical care, information, and antibiotics.

Medical science with all its knowledge is inadequate to take care of the world's venereal disease problem. Yet millenniums before the microscope, and before man knew the method of the transmission of venereal diseases, God knew all about them and gave to man the only feasible plan of preventing these universal and blighting killers. Jesus clearly stated that, from the beginning, our Father ordained that one man and one woman should constitute a family unit.[17] This plan of two, and two alone, constituting a family unit is so unique, so different from human plans, and so effective in the prevention of the vast complications of horrible venereal diseases, that again we are forced to recognize another medical evidence of the inspiration of the Bible.

CHAPTER 7

The Enemies of Sexual Happiness

EVERYONE REMEMBERS THE STORY OF THE PIED PIPER OF Hamelin who enticed the younger set to follow the enchanting, irresistible music of his flute. He led the children into a cave in a mountain, and they were never seen again.

Each generation produces a swarm of pied pipers. In the middle of this century one of them swung down the main streets of America, playing the catchy tune of "sex freedom." His sprightly, jazzy jingles promised emancipation from the "traditions" and "horrible confinement of religious inhibitions." There were many who left their homes and loved ones to race down the street after this alluring music. The piper had neither flute nor the waving hips of a rock-and-roll singer. He was a zoologist who gathered certain statistics on the theme of sex, and he shook them and beat upon them like a tambourine.

First, let us look at the statistics he gathered.[1] He and his associates had interviewed 5,940 women, questioning them about the intimate details of their past and present sexual lives. From these reports, our piper figured the percentages of the women engaged in this and that sexual perversion, the percentages of those who had had premarital experiences, and the percentages of those who were guilty of extramarital affairs. From these percentages he drew certain conclusions.

Authorities and specialists have taken exception to this report and to the conclusions that Dr. Alfred C. Kinsey made. In the first place, Kinsey interviewed only one out of every fourteen thousand women in the country. Second, these women were certainly not typical of the average American woman, because in this abnormal sampling the ratio of single women to married women was three times greater than that found in the country at large, and the ratio of college women to noncollege women was ten times greater. Third, the only women in the group were women who had volunteered to lay bare the details of their intimate sexual lives. Such women are rare in more ways than one. Women who would volunteer to reveal such sexual secrets would' be women who had, probably as a result of their sexual experiences, lost an inborn feminine reticence. Many of these women stated that they enjoyed being bitten during the sex act, and that trait certainly marks them as being abnormal. It is a neurotic mind that can translate pain into pleasure.

Kinsey's sampling was loaded with atypical and masochistic women. It was the sexual image of this group of women—who were strangely devoid of the natural inhibitions of women—that was superimposed on all other women.

There are a number of other faults in the Kinsey report. First, it is inferred that if the "average woman" is engaged in an act, then that act is advisable. There is a gulf as wide as the Grand Canyon between that which is *advisable* and that which is *average*. The average Hindu drinks filthy water on his pilgrimages, but it is certainly not advisable, since the Hindus die of cholera by the thousands. The faulty implication in the Kinsey report is that it is advisable for women to adjust to that which is average, even to a badly distorted average.

Second, having classified a woman and a hog in the same zoological category, Kinsey could see no reason why a woman's sexual life should not be patterned after that of a hog. A hog has no horrible inhibitions about sex; why should a woman?

Many people thought the reasoning seemed plausible, smacking as it did of science. After all, they asked themselves, had not "certain skilled psychiatrists" told Kinsey that restraints were bad for the mind? Now, if men and women mingled freely in the pen of promiscuity, the ultimate in living could be achieved. There would be no restraints and no frustrations. Here at last was the panacea that could cure all their longings. People could disregard the Biblical warnings against fornication, adultery, homosexuality, and other perversions.[2] They could follow the piper of promiscuity into a Utopia where nary a restriction would be placed on sexual impulses, however wild and bizarre they might be.

This zoologist deplored the fact that the "outdated laws" of the moral code were a great hindrance to the operation of his ideas. But modern pipers feel that these laws will soon be changed. Until they are, they suggest that their followers seek "to avoid open conflict with the law." I suppose rape of little girls and defenseless women should not be attempted if there were the probability of conflict with the law.

Is it not a little strange that a zoologist, a specialist in animals, should set himself up as an authority on the sex life of women? Dealing with the purely animal aspects of the matter, he fails completely to realize the deeply human relationships involved.

What do medical specialists think about putting women and hogs in the same sexual category? Two specialists, a gynecologist and a psychiatrist, resented this bull-in-the-china-shop intrusion so strongly that they wrote a book to refute Kinsey's erroneous statements. Here is a little of their thought:

Kinsey argues that inasmuch as all types of sexual behavior occur in subhuman species, these patterns are normal for humans. This kind of logic disregards all the ethical, religious, and moral advances mankind has made. . . . Kinsey also abandons the whole medical concept of perversions and puts heterosexuality on the same level as homosexuality and animal contact. . . . The healthy sex act consists of very complex psychological phenomena. It depends on the spiritual merger of one personality with another. The sex impulse in humans is tied to the deepest emotions. . . . Love simply cannot be measured on an IBM machine. Orgasm per se means nothing.[3]

Kinsey assured his followers that the spread of venereal diseases through premarital intercourse is "a relatively unimportant matter today."[4] This salesman of promiscuity is at variance with the U.S. Public Health Service which recently reported: "We estimate the reservoir of untreated syphilitics today at 1,200,000 cases and that the true

annual incidence is 60,000 cases."[5] It has been further
estimated that the annual number of new cases of gonorrhea in this country is 1,000,000 cases.

Kinsey is far removed from the best medical opinions
when he makes repeated inferences that girls who engage
in premarital petting have more successful marriages than
those who do not.[6] Medical specialists, who deal with
people rather than animals, refute his deduction:

Such advice is scientifically wrong. There is no premium
for premarital petting to orgasm. There are no penalties
for not indulging in this manner. Experience proves that
neurotic girls are the most persistent petters and that emotionally healthy girls usually reject sex without love.
Successful marriage and sexual adjustment are based more
on gradually established confidence, liking and mutual
respect than on any premarital trial and error sexual
process.[7]

A reviewer of a book written by medical experts states
in the *Journal of the American Medical Association:*

The authors justly allege that Kinsey has discussed many
difficult medical problems without the medical knowledge
and clinical experience necessary to an understanding of
the principles involved, that he has vitally overlooked the
profound influence of the psychological aspects of sexual
behavior, and that, without training and experience in
psychiatry, he has exhibited an utter disregard of the sexual
neuroses with their multifaceted evil effects.[8]

Dr. J. Irving Sands of the Neurological Institute of New
York also disagrees with Dr. Kinsey:

My own experience in dealing with many neurotic and
psychotic people . . . has led me to conclude that premarital sexual activity by females leaves a blight on the
emotional part of their personality. Moreover, these activities are a source of emotional conflict.[9]

All of which reminds me of a sign I once saw in a department store: "Slightly Used. Greatly Reduced in Price."

Before any of us are tempted to listen to this pied piper,
it might be smart to look at the fate of those who have
already followed him. Enough human guinea pigs, geared
to the idea that *newness* is synonymous with *superiority,*

have already raced down the street after him, so that an honest-to-goodness appraisal can be made.

An outstanding New York City psychoanalyst, Dr. Eugene Eisner, tells of a patient who was certainly not frustrated by any "horrible religious inhibitions," yet in 1950 the patient reported, "I've had six love affairs since 1940, but I can't seem to enjoy any of it. Is there something the matter with me? I feel that I am not getting out of sex what I'm supposed to."[10]

Another psychiatrist states, "For about fifteen years I have been the confidant of Broadway and Hollywood actors and actresses who have opportunities to live a promiscuous sexual life. And some of them live it to the hilt—eight, ten, twelve 'affairs' a year. But when they trust you and let down their hair, they will confess how frustrating and unsatisfying it all is."[11]

Into a health clinic in San Francisco landed two thousand girls who had been enthralled by the flutes, hips and statistics of a variety of pied pipers. These girls were asked if they had obtained even transitory pleasure from their sexual experiences. According to the advocates of sexual freedom, one would expect an enthusiastic affirmative. On the contrary, only a third of the girls reported "some pleasure." The other two thirds described their feelings as those of "doubt, guilt, shame, indifference, or definitely unpleasant."[12]

It should ever be remembered that it is God who created sex urges in men and women, and God put His stamp of approval on marriage. "Marriage is honourable in all, and the bed undefiled: but whoremongers and adulterers God will judge."[13] The restraints in God's Guidebook were never designed to diminish man's sexual enjoyment but rather to enable him to achieve maximal pleasure in this area. Pathetic indeed that many people are like cows who break through a fence surrounding their lush pasturage and then live on starvation rations in a desert of cactus.

Howard Whitman, American journalist who traveled extensively to study the human products of this neosexuality, writes:

New standards of sex freedom have been tried, bringing new highs of illegitimacy, a crushing burden of divorce, and a greater psychiatric caseload than ever. . . . the old formula has been flouted and the "new freedom" has failed. Youth has been hurt badly. There are the kind of hurts we know about, when social agencies and the law step in and file their reports on pregnancies, forced marriages, and venereal disease. There are the hushed-up hurts, when distraught families manage "to keep quiet." And there are the silent hurts, when youth is "lucky," manages to "get away with it." These silent hurts—the remorse, the regrets, the loss of self-respect, the blight upon the individual's future life—can be the greatest hurts of all.[14]

As a physician I have had some experience with these various hurts. Many a young girl has dampened my desk with her tears. The shame, the disgrace, and the ostracism brand her, and the pain often lasts through many years. A great variety of resulting neurotic manifestations can produce any of the many psychosomatic diseases. The community does not know, but the physician knows, that breaking through God's fences around sex is the basic cause of Kathy's toxic goiter, or Helen's arthritis, or Suzanne's commitment to an insane asylum. True, these girls were not bound by the "horrible confinement of religious inhibitions." But they experienced confinements of different sorts—and much, much harder to bear. The promised "sex freedom" turned out to be unbearable slavery of the worst sort.

The real enemies of man's sexual happiness are those who would entice him away from his home, his family, and the Biblical standards. Few people have ever stopped to realize that the blessings of sex and civilization that we enjoy exist because a large proportion of people take heed of the words of Jesus: "But from the beginning of the creation, God made them male and female. For this cause shall a man leave his father and mother, and cleave to his wife; And they twain shall be one flesh: so then they are no more twain, but one flesh."[15]

People who take this Scriptural standard as their model will save themselves from many diseases and a thousand heartaches. It is refreshing to see outstanding specialists recognize that the Biblical standard of marriage surpasses all human plans. Addressing an annual meeting of New York State physicians, Dr. Irving J. Sands said:

It may be well to call attention to the fact that change and progress are not synonymous and all that is new is not necessarily good, nor all that is old necessarily bad. . . . The Ten Commandments are old indeed, and yet they comprise the greatest mental hygiene code and the best set of rules and regulations for ethical human relationships ever produced by mankind. . . . A happy marriage is the result of a harmonious relationship between two mature people. Marriage is the greatest institution of civilized man.[16]

CHAPTER 8

The Superlatives in Sex

"DOCTOR, I CAN'T SLEEP, AND I CAN'T ENJOY ANYTHING any more. I know when my trouble began—when Gil started to play cards with a bunch of fellows. They don't gamble, but they go out one night every single week to an expensive hotel for a big steak dinner. Then they play cards until one or two in the morning. Everything is on the up and up, but—"

Pretty Mrs. Gilbert Steiner choked a bit and then continued. "Oh, I know I'm foolish. But still, here is the way I look at it. With our five children, we have to watch every penny to make ends meet. I've told Gil that I get tired and nervous staying home month in and month out. I've asked him to take me out to the movies or to dinner once in a while, but he always says there is no money for that and a babysitter, too. But he takes the little money we could use for recreation and spends it on himself. As a result there is considerable tension between us, and we aren't enjoying each other at all."

Here was a marriage falling apart because an important cohesive had been lost. The password to a happy marriage is *together*—live together, play together, work together, think together and plan together. Two people can not be held together long unless there is some sort of binding force, and sexuality is a short-lived binder, as the sex marriages of Hollywood have long demonstrated. Because sex is the only cohesive that many couples know anything about, it is not strange that about one out of every three marriages falls apart.

There is one binder that has never failed to hold two people together—love. "Love never fails." This love is not the "puppy love" played up in novels and on TV. What is love, the element so essential to every happy marriage?

Although most people understand the meaning of sexuality, few have a clear conception of what is love. The vagueness concerning love is evidenced by the fact that the dictionary gives eight different definitions. In this chapter I wish to discuss only the meaning of love as *an outward reach of the mind to help and please others. Love in this meaning of the word is not sexual, yet this kind of love must be present if the superlatives are to be obtained from sex.* The superlatives in sex—the best, the most, and for the longest time—are only possible when thoughtfulness, consideration and love for others exist.

Mr. Guy Bullom is continents away from the superlatives when he blatantly asserts that he is going "to look after No. 1," both in his business and his sex life. He perpetually berates his wife for her faults, yet he can't understand why she doesn't exhibit enthusiasm for him and his approaches. Although he has had several "affairs" with his secretaries, he fails to realize why none of them satisfied him. Variety and frequency is a mocking substitute for quality, and Mr. Bullom knows nothing of that superlative—the best.

This highly-sexed, egocentric individual gets practically nothing out of sex for the simple reason that he is sadly lacking in love. As a result he is always disappointed and frustrated sexually. His resentments toward others are largely responsible for boosting his blood pressure to 240/110. Many are the nights the poor fellow sits in a chair, wheezing through the long hours with his asthma, which is often triggered by emotional upsets.

Dr. Carl Jung recognized the underlying reason why many a man like Guy Bullom has such illnesses and such an unhappy existence: "It arises from his having no love, but only sexuality . . . and no understanding, because he has failed to read the meaning of his own existence."[1]

There are countless unhappy marriages, devoid of sexual fulfillment, because the couples do not know the difference between love and sexuality. The only love they know is something pictured in novels, torrid magazines, movies and TV. Because some couples know only "puppy love," it is no wonder they lead "a dog's life."

Yvonne was that kind of a person. She put her head on my desk and sobbed. After awhile she blurted out, "I was only kidding when I said something about Mike's mother. But he got mean and said something awful about my mother. Then I slapped him good and hard across his face. Just what he deserved! But the big brute up and punched me in the face. Look at my eye! I'm moving out! I'm taking my two kids and going back to Mom's. I love Mike, but I can't take this!"

Then, as Yvonne held an ice bag over her left eye and looked at me with the other, I gave her a little marriage counseling, somewhat belated to be sure. I ended my lecture with words something like these: "Yvonne, in every marriage, situations are bound to arise in which one of the partners must give in, out of consideration and love for the other partner. Don't feel sorry for yourself if you discover that you are the one who has to give in most of the time. I have strange but good news for you: when you give in to Mike, you are losing your life in the one and only way to find life and worthwhile happiness. The secret of happiness in married life depends on each partner making small sacrifices, readily and cheerfully.

"You say you have love for Mike. Is it the kind of love that suffers long and is kind? The only love that will stand the acid test of everyday living is that which God describes and gives to those who walk in the light of His commandments: 'Love is patient; love is kind and envies no one. Love is never boastful, nor conceited, nor rude; never selfish, not quick to take offence. Love keeps no scores of wrongs. . . . There is nothing love cannot face; there is no limit to its faith, its hope, and its endurance. Love will never come to an end.' "[2]

Love is a basic necessity, not only for obtaining the superlatives of sex but also for living. Dr. Smiley Blanton, in his recent book *Love or Perish*, says: "For more than forty years I have sat in my office and listened while people of all ages and classes told me of their hopes and fears. . . . As I look back over the long, full years, one truth emerges clearly in my mind—the universal need for love. . . . They cannot survive without love; they must have it or they will perish."[3]

Many couples are not happy. They go through the

motions of sex but have no sexual fulfillment. If they have other affairs, their frustrations only increase. They hardly ever sense that the feelings they long for can only be obtained where love for one another exists. There can be no real ecstasy unless the sex act expresses a love and intense awareness of the needs and desires of the other. Wrangling during the day will make sex lifeless and mechanical, if not repulsive.

Frustrated couples often think there must be something wrong with their sex departments, so they go off to a psychiatrist for help. Fortunate they are if they go to one who gives them advice such as psychoanalyst Erich Fromm offers:

There is no more convincing proof that the injunction, "Love thy neighbor as thyself," is the most important norm of living and that its violation is the basic cause of unhappiness and mental illness than the evidence gathered by the psychoanalyst. Whatever complaints the . . . patient may have, whatever symptoms he may present, are rooted in his inability to love, if we mean by love a capacity for the experience of concern, responsibility, respect and understanding of another person and an intense desire for that other person's growth. Analytic therapy is essentially an attempt to help the patient gain or regain his capacity for love. If this aim is not fulfilled, nothing but surface changes can be accomplished.[4]

Love is as essential to happiness and mental health as is food to our physical well-being. Men particularly fail to comprehend that sex alone is inadequate nourishment for a happy marriage. Orgasm in men is almost a purely mechanical act, while in women it is much more complex. A woman must be fully aware of the man's thoughtfulness for her, of his fidelity to her, and of his love that puts her pleasure ahead of his own.

Psychiatrist Max Levin recognized that unselfish love is necessary for obtaining the superlatives in sex: "It is obvious, then, that maturity is a prerequisite for a happy marriage. In the immature state of infancy there is no obligation to give. The infant *receives;* he is not expected to do anything else. The success of a marriage will depend in great degree on the extent to which the partners have outgrown their infantile dependency and achieved the capacity to assume responsibility, to wish more to give than to receive."[5]

Centuries before Yvonne and Mike had their childish quarrel, and centuries before the birth of modern psychiatry, the Bible showed the necessity of displacing immaturity with love and thus gave a splendid prescription for a happy marriage: "When I was a child, my speech, my outlook, and my thoughts were all childish. When I grew up, I had finished with childish things. . . . In a word, there are three things that last forever: faith, hope, and love; but the greatest of them all is love."[6]

The love that is thoughtful and unselfish makes life's greatest dream come to pass, but sex without love can make of life a horrible nightmare. One of many who discovered this truth the hard way was the prodigal son.[7] His was the voice of immaturity: "Give me." He, like many today, hastened into a country far removed from his father's precepts and there wasted the endowments of money and body "with riotous living." His soul became an empty void inhabited only by haunting echoes. He hit bottom in one of life's pigpens where he yearned to eat the empty husks that the hogs were crunching. He discovered that sex in a country removed from God's will is empty, disappointing and ugly. Self-gratification is ever a one-way street—with a hogpen at the end.

As the young man remembered that his father's house always had "bread enough and to spare," he discovered that "the horrible religious inhibitions" were not as bad as he had been led to believe. He began to sense that there is a close relationship between proper inhibitions and abundant blessings.

When he had left home, his immaturity was evidenced by his attitude of "Give me." When he returned, repenting, the spirit of *"Give me"* was absent. In its place was thoughtfulness for others—*"Make me a servant."*

How important is the matter of sex in the marriage relationship? Dr. Emil Novak, of Johns Hopkins Medical School, states convincingly that "There are many women who are physically and emotionally normal, who love their husbands devotedly, who have borne children, yet have never throughout their married lives experienced any great degree of physical satisfaction from the sex act. Nor do they feel frustrated or cheated."[8]

In fact, some authorities state that less than half of married women have ever experienced sexual orgasm. However, the emotions they derive from the sexual act are beautiful and completely gratifying without any need for physical climax. Their emotions are diffused throughout their bodies. To them the glowing embers of hardwood are just as satisfying as the quick bright flash of a little gunpowder.

Because of their ignorance of these facts, many young women develop frustrations and resentments that tragically worsen the marital situation. If thoughtfulness for one another predominates, then these same women will experience increasingly greater satisfaction from the marital relationship. Possession of God-given love will prevent frustrations, unhappiness and divorce, with their long trains of mental and physical diseases.

Someone has said: "The cure for all the ills and wrongs, the cares, the sorrows and the crimes of humanity, all lie in one word 'love.' It is the divine vitality that everywhere produces and restores life. To each and every one of us, it gives the power of working miracles if we will."

How is this *summum bonum* obtained and maintained? It is obtained in its fullest measure when God, who is Love, comes to indwell the man or woman who opens the door of the heart. Nothing less than the divine indwelling will suffice when the individual finds himself in the strong current of sexual temptation.

This love is maintained by obediently following the leadings of the Word and the Spirit. There is no valid reason for the Christian to succumb to a host of diseases, for the promise of God is sure: "There hath no temptation taken you but such as is common to man: but God is faithful, who will not suffer you to be tempted above that ye are able; but will with the temptation also make a way to escape, that ye may be able to bear it."[9]

CHAPTER 9

Upset Mind—Sick Body

SIX-YEAR-OLD HELEN SEIBERT, SITTING ON HER MOTHER'S lap, eyed me like a scared rabbit. Her mother answered my inquiring look: "Doctor, Helen has been vomiting every day for six weeks. Nearly everything I give her comes up. She began to vomit the day after Labor Day."

The day after Labor Day was the time Helen began to attend the large central school with its hundreds of new, strange faces. This experience was indeed overwhelming to her because she lived far up Turtle Creek where children were few.

Why was she vomiting? Her fear of the many strangers had sent hurried impulses along nerves from her emotional center to tighten the muscular outlet of her stomach. As a result much of her food could not pass into the intestines and was regurgitated. Little Helen had lost a great deal of weight.

I suggested that she remain home for a week. There was no more vomiting. Then the better-adjusted Helen returned to school and had no further trouble.

Such trouble is not confined to children. On a Saturday night, eighteen-year-old Donna Cole told me she had been vomiting and suffering from severe abdominal cramps and diarrhea for five days. Her trouble had begun about an hour after she had left the dentist's office.

The dentist had told this pretty, popular girl that she must have all of her teeth pulled and be fitted with false ones. Result: a tempest in her emotional center. Nerve impulses from this center quickly initiated and perpetuated vomiting, severe cramps, and diarrhea. Donna was greatly surprised when I told her that the cause of the trouble was not in her abdomen but above her ears.

Equally surprised was Elaine Johnson when she discovered that her headaches came from anxiety about losing her boyfriend. Bill Landry found out that that it was not the professor's assignment that gave him asthma, but his griping about it. Hal Stevens could not understand why his diabetes flared out of control after he took that "stupid test." And the professor who gave the test could not see how his arthritis became so much worse after he corrected the test papers.

These cases illustrate the most intriguing subject in modern medicine. With every passing year, we obtain a wider comprehension of the ability of the mind (*psyche*) to produce varied disturbances in the body (*soma*): hence the term *psychosomatic*. Invisible emotional tension in the mind can produce striking visible changes in the body, changes that can become serious and fatal.

This concept should give us a new perspective on conditions that are often contemptuously referred to as "being in the head." Obviously such conditions as vomiting, diarrhea, asthma, diabetes, and deformed arthritic joints are not "in the head," yet these and scores of other serious diseases are triggered by tension in the mind.

What percentage of a physician's practice is made up of patients whose symptoms and bodily diseases are caused by emotional turmoil? Statistics reported in 1948 indicated that two thirds of the patients who went to a physician had symptoms caused or aggravated by mental stress.[1] In 1955 an article describing the work of a leading authority on stress was published under the questioning title, "Stress the Cause of All Disease?"[2]

At the beginning of this century, bacteria were considered the center of attention. Now, fifty years later, mental stress has taken its place. In fact, experiments with animals indicated that certain bacteria could only cause disease when animals' resistance was lowered by stress.

How can certain emotions cause visible changes in the body, such as strokes of apoplexy, blindness, toxic goiters, fatal clots in the heart, bleeding ulcers of the intestinal tract, kidney diseases, and gangrene of the legs, to mention only a few of the conditions? Dr. O. Spurgeon English published an excellent, illustrated book explaining how emotions can cause debilitating and fatal illnesses.[3] The first picture in this book depicts the emotional center in the brain from which nerve fibers go out to every organ of the body. Because of the intricate nerve connections, it is understandable how any turmoil in the emotional center can send out impulses which can cause anything from a headache to itching in the soles of the feet.

The emotional center produces these widespread changes by means of three principal mechanisms: by changing the amount of blood flowing to an organ; by affecting the secretions of certain glands; and by changing the tension of muscles.

Emotional stress can influence the amount of blood that flows to an organ. Embarrassment can cause the blood vessels of the face and neck to open up to produce blushing, and the emotions of anxiety or hate can so increase the amount of blood within the rigid skull that headaches and vomiting result.

Irritation in the emotional center is also directed toward the glands of the body. Many of us can remember the first time we attempted to speak before an audience and we recall how parched our mouths became. Alarm messages had gone from our emotional centers, which dried up the salivary secretions. It is indeed hard to speak when the mouth is dry. Even experienced speakers may experience emotional strain and consequent drying of the saliva. Perhaps that is why a glass of water is often placed on the speaker's rostrum.

Frequently an emotional tempest sends S.O.S. messages to the thyroid gland for its secretions. When an excess of thyroxin is poured into the blood over a long period, the symptoms of toxic goiter are seen: extreme nervousness, bulging eyes, rapid pulse, and even fatal heart disease.

Emotional tension affects the secretion of the ovaries in a variety of ways. Disturbance of these glands can cause a cessation of the menses, pain at the time of the period, or an upset before the period characterized by irritableness, headaches, and bloating.

The highly important adrenal glands are frequently the target of emotional fire. Their secretions in abnormal amounts can cause high blood pressure, arthritis, kidney disease, and hardening of the arteries—the last killer alone is responsible for the annual slaughter of 800,000 in the United States.

Emotional stress can affect the tone of the muscles. All of us have felt our muscles tightening up when we became frightened or angry. Tightened muscles can produce pain, as one can demonstrate by clenching a fist for a few minutes. Hence, it is understandable why people with chronic anxieties suffer a great deal with severe tension headaches that stem from tightened neck muscles.

The involuntary muscles of the intestines can also be affected. As an example, consider the initial landing of our paratroopers during the invasion of France in World War II. As the men slowly floated down in their parachutes, German bullets screeched all around them. Consider how you would have felt if you had been up there! Consider the rapid messages that went from their emotional centers to the muscles of their intestines.

Emotional turmoil can also manifest itself through pain over the heart. One day I received an urgent call to see a student who was "dying from a heart attack." I found him on the floor, gasping for breath and suffering real pain over his heart. He presented almost the same picture as a person dying from heart trouble, but he was in no danger at all.

He was a freshman at the college and was having difficulty adjusting to the tempo of college life. The pain over his heart was as real as a pain from a broken rib; it was not caused by a diseased heart, but by a troubled emotional center.

During World War I men with such a condition were great liabilities in the army. When World War II came along, special efforts were made to weed out such men. In fact, ten times as many men were rejected for this emotional type of heart pain as for all other heart diseases. Plenty of it was seen too among the civilian population after every bombing of English cities, when tens of thousands were unable to go to work because of chest pains.

Even in peace times, it constitutes one of the most common conditions seen in a physician's office. I think now of a very fine man who, with pain over his heart and gasping for breath, has often been speeded in an ambulance to a hospital. Expensive hospitalization and tests always indicate that his trouble originates in emotional upsets. Frightening and incapacitating as these attacks are, they are not dangerous.

However, fatal heart attacks can be triggered by "anger in all degrees, depression, and anxiety," according to Dr. Roy R. Grinker, one of the medical directors of Michael Reese Hospital in Chicago. This doctor states that anxiety places more stress on the heart than any other stimulus, including physical exercise and fatigue.[4]

The influence of emotional stress on the human body can be demonstrated by a partial listing of diseases it causes or aggravates. Of course it should not be assumed that the emotional factor is the sole cause in any of these cases:

Disorders of the Digestive System
  Ulcers of the mouth, stomach, and intestines
  Ulcerative and mucous colitis
  Loss of appetite
  Hiccoughs
  Constipation
  Diarrhea

Disorders of the Circulatory System
  High blood pressure
  Soldier's heart
  Paroxysmal tachycardia
  Arteriosclerosis
  Coronary thrombosis
  Gangrene of legs
  Rheumatic fever
  Cerebral strokes of apoplexy

Disorders of the Genito-Urinary System
  Painful menstruation
  Lack of menstruation
  Premenstrual tension and irritability
  Frigidity and vaginismus
  Painful coitus
  Frequent and painful urination
  Acute glomerular nephritis (kidney disease)
  Menopausal symptoms
  Impotence

Disorders of the Nervous System
  Headaches of several types
  Alcoholism
  Epilepsy
  Psychoneuroses
  Insanities such as schizophrenia
  Senile dementia

Disorders of Glands of Internal Secretion
  Hyperthyroidism
  Diabetes
  Obesity

Allergic Disorders
  Hives
  Hay fever
  Asthma

Muscle-Joint Disorders
  Backache
  Pain and spasm of muscles
  Rheumatoid arthritis
  Osteoarthritis

Infections
  Infectious mononucleosis
  Polio
  Many, perhaps all, infections

Eye Diseases
  Glaucoma
  Keratitis

Skin Diseases
  Hives
  Atopic dermatitis
  Neurodermatitis
  Raynaud's disease
  Scleroderma
  Lupus erythematosus disseminata
  Psoriasis

CHAPTER 10

It's Not What You Eat
—It's What Eats You

BIG BILL BRANDON WAS A VERY LIKABLE FELLOW—WHEN he didn't "go off at the handle." When one of his men at the plant messed up an assignment, Bill would get furious and throw at him the sharpest epithets in his voluminous but unprintable vocabulary. But the abuse he hurled at the other fellow always seemed to boomerang on poor Bill and eventually put him in bed.

Then his wife would call me to the house. It was such an old story that she would merely open the door and

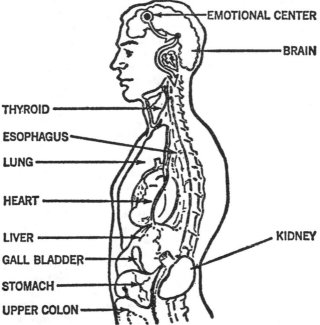

SELF-CENTEREDNESS   ENVY   JEALOUSY   RESENTMENT
HATE   WORRY   OVERSENSITIVITY   GUILT FEELINGS
FEAR   SORROW   DESIRE FOR APPROVAL   FRUSTRATION

EMOTIONAL CENTER
BRAIN
THYROID
ESOPHAGUS
LUNG
HEART
LIVER
KIDNEY
GALL BLADDER
STOMACH
UPPER COLON

ULCERS OF STOMACH AND INTESTINE   COLITIS
HIGH BLOOD PRESSURE   HEART TROUBLE   STROKES
ARTERIOSCLEROSIS   KIDNEY DISEASE   HEADACHES
MENTAL DISTURBANCES   GOITER   DIABETES   ARTHRITIS

Effects of Emotions on Physical Health

give a broad sweep of her hand toward Bill's bedroom with a laconic shrug of her shoulders and a forced smile. "Doc, he has been vomiting two weeks straight, but he wouldn't let me call you until this morning."

One couldn't help feeling sorry for big Bill as he lay

on his stomach in bed. His eyes were big, red, desperate and pleading for help. Of course, he had been studied and X rayed in several hospitals, where he had spent a small fortune. His trouble was always brought on by anger, which tightened the outlet of his stomach and caused the intractable vomiting. The occurrences were so frequent and severe that Bill was having a hard time working enough to support his wife and eight children.

Bill's stomach must have had a stainless steel lining, because after such a build-up of acid in the stomach most people develop ulcers, if not cancer. In fact, it is generally agreed in medical circles that ulcers are caused not so much by what the person eats as by "what eats" the person. Of course, after ulcers develop they are aggravated by certain foods and emotional upsets.

Another picture in Dr. English's book portrays the emotions that can cause a tightening of the muscular outlet of the stomach. Fear, love need (need for security), and sorrow will be taken up in later chapters. Also pictured are jealousy, envy, self-centeredness, ambition, frustration, rage, resentment and hatred. Observe that these disease-producing emotions are concerned with protecting and coddling the self, and they could be summarized under one title—*self-centeredness.*

Centuries before modern psychiatry discovered that carnal emotions were important factors in the causation of many psychosomatic diseases, the Bible condemned these emotions and provided a cure for them: "The activities of the lower nature are obvious. Here is a list: sexual immorality, . . . hatred, quarrelling, jealousy, bad temper, rivalry, factions, party-spirit, envy, drunkenness, orgies and things like that . . .";[1] "Those who belong to Christ Jesus have crucified the flesh with its emotions and passions."[2]

Dr. William Sadler was also impressed by the close connection between the sinful "activities of the lower nature" and many diseases. We read:

No one can appreciate so fully as a doctor the amazingly large percentage of human disease and suffering which is directly traceable to worry, fear, conflict, immorality, dissipation, and ignorance—to unwholesome thinking and unclean living. *The sincere acceptance of the principles and teachings of Christ with respect to the life of mental peace and joy, the life of unselfish thought and clean living, would at once wipe -out more than half the difficulties, diseases, and sorrows of the human race.* In other words, more than one half of the present affliction of mankind could be prevented by the tremendous prophylactic power of actually living up to the personal and practical spirit of the real teachings of Christ.

The teachings of Jesus applied to our modern civilization—understandingly applied, not merely nominally accepted—would so purify, uplift, and vitalize us that the race would immediately stand out as a new order of beings, possessing superior mental power and increased moral force. Irrespective of the future rewards of living, laying aside all discussion of future life, *it would pay any man or woman to live the Christ-life just for the mental and moral rewards it affords here in this present world.* Some day man may awake to the fact that the teachings of Christ are potent and powerful in preventing and curing disease. Some day our boasted scientific development, as regards mental and moral improvement, may indeed catch up with the teachings of this man of Galilee.[8]

Shakespeare knew enough of the Bible and psychiatry to recognize that people can become sick from unconfessed sin. It was the memory of the murder of Duncan that produced psychosomatic overtones in Lady Macbeth. When Macbeth asked the physician about her illness, he replied:

> "No so sick, my lord,
> As she is troubled with thick-coming fancies,
> That keep her from her rest."[4]

The doctor was then asked the same question put to many a physician today:

> Canst thou not minister to mind diseas'd,
> Pluck from the memory a rooted sorrow,
> Raze out the written troubles of the brain,
> And with some sweet oblivious antidote
> Cleanse the stuff'd bosom of that perilous stuff
> Which weighs upon the heart?[5]

A man about forty years of age came into my office one evening. His stomach was bothering him and he could not sleep. It seemed as though he might have to give up his job and would be unable to support his family of three. When he came into my office, I did not detect any bodily ailment, but I recognized that he was on the verge of a serious nervous breakdown.

After telling me about some of the things that he felt had caused his trouble, he said, "Doctor, I have done other things that would put me behind bars."

I recognized that we were dealing with something far beyond the reach of a tranquilizer. I told him so and advised him to bow his head on my desk, confess, and ask his heavenly Father for forgiveness.

He did just that, simply and earnestly. Immediately and miraculously God removed "that perilous stuff, which weighs upon the heart." Several years have passed, and the man has not lost a day from his work. He is happy and buoyant. His trouble had not been caused by anything he was eating; it had stemmed from elements gnawing at his vitals.

Psychiatrist Sadler writes, "A clear conscience is a great step toward barricading the mind against neuroticism." Psychologist Henry C. Link also sees the connection between sin and disease: "The emphasis on sin has largely disappeared from the teachings of religion . . . at the very time when psychology has discovered its importance and extended its meaning."[6]

One may ask, "If an individual is converted and crucifies everything in his life that is contrary to God's Word, will that individual then be free of the diseases caused by jealousy, envy, self-centeredness, resentment and hatred?"

An episode about a person I know might answer that question. The woman was a missionary in India and under great burden for the immoral conditions that existed there. She prayed about them, but spent many an hour lamenting to her husband and others about the deplorable conditions. Let us assume she was justified in resenting the people responsible for the state of affairs; but the point is, *she did resent them.*

Her resentment tightened up the muscular ring at the outlet of her stomach, and she developed an ulcer. One day that ulcer began to bleed and it bled for about six days until that woman was almost exsanguinated. Here was a fine Christian woman who loved the Lord, who had crucified self, and was in full-time service for the Lord. Yet she developed an ulcer and nearly died from hemorrhage.

By changing a few details, the same story could be told of tens of thousands of professed Christians who, instead of bleeding ulcers, come down with one of the psychosomatic diseases already listed. Consecrations made at an altar are not sufficient. There must be a daily crucifixion of self, and obedience to all of God's commandments, if one is to be freed from these diseases.

Furthermore, human beings are not perfect in knowledge. We can still make errors in judgment and in attitudes toward others. Verily, verily, in proportion as we understand and obey the directions in the Guidebook we shall be blessed in mind and body.

Applicable here is an admonition from the Letter to the Hebrews: "Let it be your ambition to live at peace with all men and to achieve holiness 'without which no man shall see the Lord.' Be careful that none of you fails to respond to the grace which God gives, for if he does there can very easily spring up in him a bitter spirit which is not only bad in itself but can also poison the lives of many others."[7]

What a person eats is not as important as the bitter spirit, the hates, and the feelings of guilt that eat at him. A dose of baking soda in the stomach will never reach these acids that destroy body, mind and soul.

The Bible doesn't merely treat the disease-producing factors of envy, self-centeredness, resentment, hatred and immorality, but it strikes at the cause with an effective and curative manner: "Those who belong to Christ have crucified their old nature with all that it loved and lusted for."[8]

CHAPTER 11

"The High Cost of Getting Even"

I RECEIVED MUCH INSPIRATION FOR THIS CHAPTER FROM Dale Carnegie's account of a trip to Yellowstone Park and a visit to the place where the grizzly bears are fed.[1] He did not have to wait long before a grizzly bear came into a clearing where garbage had been dumped to entice him. The guide told the group that the grizzly bear can whip any animal in the West with the possible exceptions of the buffalo and Kadiak bear. That night, as Dale Carnegie sat with the other tourists in the bleachers, he noticed that there was only one animal the grizzly would allow to eat with him—a *skunk*. Of course, the grizzly could have won in any fight with a skunk. He resented the skunk and yearned to get even with him for his brazen impudence. But he didn't. Why? Because he knew there would be *the high cost of getting even*.

Smart grizzly! Certainly much smarter than many human beings who spend weary days and sleepless nights brooding over their resentments and trying to hatch ways to squelch someone. Man doesn't ever seem to learn that the high cost of getting even may be toxic goiter, strokes of apoplexy, and fatal heart attacks.

One day a man came into my office with his fourteen-year-old boy. The father said to me, "I only came to get some more pills for my wife's colitis."

Immediately the youngster asked, "Well, Dad, who has Ma been colliding with now?"

Is there any connection between this distressing diarrhea of blood and mucous and our "colliding" with people and then trying to get even? The preponderance of evidence favors the view that a disordered emotional life is the primary disturbance in cases of colitis. Flare-ups of mucous colitis can often be caused and perpetuated by "collisions" with others. Two authorities on the subject write: "Murray noted that the onset and each exacerbation of the disease occurred during periods of stressful life situations. Many investigators have corroborated his findings. Experimental studies have demonstrated the relationship between life stress and ulceration of the colonic mucosa of man."[2]

A study at one hospital revealed, through personal interviews with patients suffering from mucous colitis, that resentment was the most prominent personality characteristic, occurring in ninety-six per cent of the victims.[3]

The more serious ulcerative colitis also can be caused by emotional turmoil. The ulcers in the colon can truly plague the sufferer, who often gets little help from any medication. The only surgical procedure of any avail is the surgical removal of the colon and entire rectum, a high price to pay for getting even with an enemy.

For centuries scoffers have ridiculed the advice of Jesus, "Love your enemies," as being impractical, idealistic and absurd. Now psychiatrists are recommending it as a panacea for many of man's ills.

When Jesus said, "Forgive seventy-times seven," He was thinking not only of our souls, but of saving our bodies from ulcerative colitis, toxic goiters, high blood pressure, and scores of other diseases. The advice of the Great Physician appears to have percolated even into the hard-boiled bulletin of a Milwaukee police department. "If selfish people try to take advantage of you, cross them off your list, but don't try to get even. When you try to get even, you hurt yourself more than you hurt the other fellow."[4]

Booker T. Washington, who became famous in spite of prejudice against his color, and who was insulted times without number, wrote, "I will not let any man reduce my soul to the level of hatred."

The famous physiologist, John Hunter, knew what anger could do to his heart: "The first scoundrel that gets me angry will kill me." Some time later, at a medical meeting, a speaker made assertions that incensed Hunter. As he stood up and bitterly attacked the speaker, his anger caused such a contraction of the blood vessels in his heart that he fell dead.

In life's frog ponds, perhaps we are able to out-croak our fellows, but it might truthfully be written on many thousands of death certificates that the victims died of "grudgitis." We have heard people say, from between clenched teeth, "I'll get even with that skunk if it's the last thing I ever do!" Too often it is exactly that.

I am reminded of a perky old lady, about eighty years old, who came to me at regular intervals to have her blood pressure checked. It usually hovered around 200, but on one particular day it soared to 230. Inwardly I was startled. However I said, calmly, "Your blood pressure is up today."

With a smile she answered, "I can easily account for that. I just had a heated argument with another patient in your waiting room."

Think of it: that cultured, intelligent woman could well have blown a cerebral "fuse" and suffered a fatal stroke, simply because she wanted to get even verbally with a man noted for his provocative chatter. Her diagnosis of the spectacular rise of her blood pressure was correct. Arguments and verbal duels cause many and aggravate all cases of high blood pressure.

The methods we use in retaliation vary. My one-year-old granddaughter, when peeved, puts out her little hands and claws the air in front of her. Some babies, when frustrated, will beat their heads against the floor. Because a baby can't see his head, it is the last part of the anatomy to be recognized as belonging to him.

Most of us cannot remember when we tried to get even with our parents by pounding our heads on the floor. However, some of us can recall how we tried to spite our parents by refusing to eat our meals. Our parents had to tell us many times that we were spiting nobody but ourselves before that obvious fact penetrated our little numbskulls.

Within the past few years, I have treated three adolescents who tried to get even with their schoolmates by punching them. None of the youngsters on the receiving end of the punches needed any medical attention, but the three boys who did the punching suffered fractures of the bones in their hands.

A few years ago I knew a college student—we shall call him Pierre—who suffered a great deal from a burning sensation and distress in his upper abdomen. I gave him the newest, most effective medication but he obtained only partial and transient relief. Going to several specialists afforded no further relief and extensive X ray studies revealed no pathology. After observing his rather tense personality pattern for several months, I felt that some emotional strain might be at the bottom of his trouble. Of course, he denied most emphatically that he was under any tension.

Pierre was a puzzle until another student told me about hearing him speak in a nearby city. Most of his talk had been devoted to a harangue describing how his grandfather had been wronged and defrauded by some people many years ago. He sought to get even with the offenders by frequent and fiery denunciations. The student who was in the audience said Pierre stood, rigid and tense as a board, and talked for over an hour, the perspiration flowing in streams down his face. Not once did he stop to wipe his face. When he finished, his collar was wilted and his shirt soaked.

When Pierre came to my office the next time I asked him again if he was under any strain or held any grudges against people. All these he denied. Then I reminded him of that talk that had been reported to me. I suggested to him that his intense desire to get even with the enemies of his grandfather was probably causing his stomach trouble. I used pictures to explain how cerebral stress can tighten up the muscular outlet of the stomach to cause indigestion. Pierre's desire for revenge was so intense that he refused to give up his resentments. Paying the price with wretched days and sleepless nights, he fattened his grudges by repeated rehearsals to every available auditor. His only concern was to learn the name of the student who had given me the information. He actually pleaded with me for that name because he wanted to give the boy a tongue lashing.

Finally, Pierre's abdominal distress bothered him so much throughout the year that his grades and personality were hurt and prevented him from returning to college.

Going up in the age scale, I recall a professional man who, when bested in an argument with his wife, would try to get even with her by grinding his teeth together. It is still a mystery to me how he thought he was spiting her by grinding and tearing the fillings out of his own teeth. That wasn't even tooth for tooth.

Many chronological years separated this man from the diaper state, yet in the area of interpersonal relationships he wasn't smarter than the vindictive baby who pounds his own head on the floor. The similarity of the two might be explained, I suppose, on the basis that they each possessed an innate carnal nature.

Most of us do not retaliate against others by pounding our heads on the floor or grinding our teeth together. Neither do we shoot one another or give doses of rat poison. That isn't Scriptural—or legal! The most common way people get even with others is by talking about them. Of course, that isn't Scriptural either, but it has the advantage of keeping us clear of the electric chair.

Running people down does not keep us free from a host of diseases of body and mind. The verbal expression of animosity toward others calls forth certain hormones from the pituitary, adrenal, thyroid, and other glands, an excess of which can cause disease in any part of the body.

Many diseases can develop when we fatten our grudges by rehearsing them in the presence of others.

The moment I start hating a man, I become his slave. I can't enjoy my work any more because he even controls my thoughts. My resentments produce too many stress hormones in my body and I become fatigued after only a few hours of work. The work I formerly enjoyed is now drudgery. Even vacations cease to give me pleasure. It may be a luxurious car that I drive along a lake fringed with the autumnal beauty of maple, oak and birch. As far as my experience of pleasure is concerned, I might as well be driving a wagon in mud and rain.

The man I hate hounds me wherever I go. I can't escape his tyrannical grasp on my mind. When the waiter serves me porterhouse steak with French fries, asparagus, crisp salad, and strawberry shortcake smothered with ice cream, it might as well be stale bread and water. My teeth chew the food and I swallow it, but the man I hate will not permit me to enjoy it.

King Solomon must have had a similar experience, for he wrote: "Better a dish of vegetables, with love, than the best beef served with hatred."[5]

The man I hate may be many miles from my bedroom; but more cruel than any slave driver, he whips my thoughts into such a frenzy that my innerspring mattress becomes a rack of torture. The lowliest of the serfs can sleep, but not I. I really must acknowledge the fact that I am a slave to every man on whom I pour the vials of my wrath.

Is it because human beings are dumber than grizzly bears that they can fill every moment in twenty-four hours with thoughts that fume like nitric acid and corrode as deeply? Or is man controlled far more than he realizes by an inner force that he recognizes and calls "Old Nick"?

I think Jesus gave the answer when James and John wanted Him to call down fire on a Samaritan village because the Samaritans wouldn't give them lodging. These disciples were believers in and followers of Jesus. Yet, mind you, these Christians, smarting from the sting of racial discrimination, were so full of carnality that they besought the Lord to call down fire on the village. The Lord rebuked them by saying, "Ye know not what manner of spirit ye are of."[6]

Before Pentecost, Peter also had an innate evil spirit.

In the Garden of Gethsemane, Peter, convulsed with fiery vengeance, tried to cut off the head of one of the opposition party. He wasn't the first or the last carnal theologian who has retaliated by cutting off heads.

What a complete transformation occurred in James, John and Peter after they crucified self and were filled with the Holy Spirit. The old spirit of getting even was replaced by the Holy Spirit of Christ who, when He was reviled, reviled not again.

The seventh chapter of Acts describes how Stephen, "being full of the Holy Spirit," reacted when he was stoned. Stoning was a horrible and painful way to kill a man, but Stephen was devoid of the spirit of revenge. Bleeding and bruised, he summoned his last bit of energy to get on his knees and pray, "Lord, lay not this sin to their charge."[7] How many of us, stoned by a vicious mob, would be primarily interested in praying with our last breath for their spiritual welfare?

We can partly answer that question by taking a little inventory. Have we been engaged in hurling back the stones that came our way? Have we, in our conversations, been trying to cut off heads or call down fire upon those who have given us a rough time? How have we reacted to some of our associates who either purposely or ignorantly did something we didn't like? Did we slam the door, refuse to go down to eat, sit and pout the rest of the evening, or run them down? An honest appraisal should make it clear whether we truly possess the Holy Spirit of Christ.

Failure to possess His Spirit will make us susceptible to many diseases of body and mind, because when we are shamefully wronged by someone, we can't resist the temptation to get even—although it means paying the high price of a pound of our own flesh. Christ can crucify the carnal spirit if we drive the spikes into everything in our lives that He marks for destruction. Then we are candidates for His baptism with the Holy Spirit.

Paul, who was convicted as he witnessed the stoning of Stephen and heard his prayer, outlines the steps toward getting rid of the disease-producing spirit of retaliation:

So put to death those members that are on earth. . . . Once you moved among them, when you lived in them; but off with them all now, off with anger, rage, malice,

slander. . . . you have stripped off the old nature with its
practices, and put on the new nature. . . . be clothed with
compassion, kindliness, humility, gentleness, and good
temper—forbear and forgive each other in any case of
complaint; as Christ forgave you, so must you forgive.
And above all you must be loving, for love is the link
of the perfect life.[8]

"None of these diseases" is the promise available to us
only if we "have stripped off the old nature with its practices" of getting even.

CHAPTER 12

Eggs—Just Eggs

"DOCTOR, MY WIFE AND I HAVE DRIVEN THIRTY MILES TO
talk with you. Neither one of us knew a sick day until a
few months ago when we developed insomnia. We both
take sleeping capsules now, sometimes two or more a
night, but we don't think that is the answer. I began to
develop pains in the pit of my stomach, but I had an
X ray and there is no trouble there. My wife started to
have pains over her heart, but a specialist examined her
and said there wasn't anything wrong. We drove over here
this afternoon to see if you could help us."

They were a pleasant looking couple in their seventies
who had retired from teaching school. I have never seen
them before. I was very busy that afternoon and was a
little nonplussed about helping them in the short time
at my disposal.

After I had asked the woman a few questions and made
a superficial examination without finding anything wrong,
she pulled a letter out of her pocket. "Doctor, you may
think I am foolish, but our troubles seemed to start right
after we got this letter. Here it is, read it.'

Dear George,
I understand that you are selling some eggs to Harry Bickerstaff. You people ought to know that I have invested considerable money in the chicken business and am able to supply more eggs to the people of this little hamlet than they can eat. You ought to know that my business is hurt by your dabbling around with a few hens and selling eggs to Harry. I think you ought to stop.

Manning Caspar

Her eyes were wet with tears when I looked up at her. She continued, "We felt we had a right to sell those eggs to Harry because he preferred our Rhode Island brown eggs to the white ones. But from that day Manning Caspar has refused to speak to us when we see him on the street. We feel terrible because we never had an experience like this. We have been upset over the whole matter. I think our whole trouble stems from—eggs—just eggs."

When she suggested that they go home and give up their egg business. I told her it might be worth a trial. Several months later the couple's daughter told me they had done just that and they had never felt so well in their lives. They stopped taking sleeping capsules and did not have an ache or a pain.

Of course, they had a perfect right to continue to sell eggs. Perhaps it was a foolish thing for them to give in to Manning Caspar. Or was it? They had already spent close to two hundred dollars for X rays and other examinations, while their profits from the eggs amounted to only a few dollars. In dollars and cents it wasn't a paying business. Besides, they were losing their peace of mind, the value of which is priceless.

I tell the following story without documentation. A friend was surprised to discover that a minister had given up his pulpit several years before and was practicing medicine. My friend asked the man why he had done it.

"I took up the practice of medicine because I discovered that people will pay more money to care for their bodies than for their souls," he answered.

Some years later the man gave up medicine and became an attorney. Perplexed, my friend again asked for a reason and received this reply: "I took up the practice of law because I discovered that people will pay more money to get their own way than for either body or soul."

How right he was! Countless people today are ruining body, mind and soul because they are bent on having their own selfish ways. Worthwhile is the saying that a man is a fool who can't be angry, but a man is wise who won't be angry.

A man and his wife avoided unhappiness, insomnia and disease because they put the inspired admonitions of God's Bible ahead of their own right to sell eggs: "And whosoever shall compel thee to go one mile, go with him two."[1] Foolish? To walk an extra mile and insure peace of mind and unbroken sleep night after night? Any of us who have done it can testify to the refreshing medical benefits we have experienced in our own bodies. Jesus, in giving this command, must have been thinking of our bodies and minds as well as our souls. "And if any man would go to law with thee, and take away thy coat, let him have thy cloak also."[2]

Such a course is hard on our pride, but it is highly beneficial to our health and happiness. Each of us must decide whether we are going to cater to our pride or to our health.

CHAPTER 13

"Love or Perish"

IN A PREVIOUS CHAPTER WE MENTIONED DR. ENGLISH'S book. In it he listed the following disease-producing emotions: jealousy, envy, self-centeredness, ambition, rage, frustration, resentment and hatred. Nineteen hundred years ago, the Apostle Paul not only warned against these emotions but also gave the antidote—love. It is coincidental, but Dr. English lists these emotions in somewhat the same order that Paul did many centuries before:

Dr. English	Apostle Paul[1]
Jealousy and envy	"love envieth not"
self-centeredness	"love vaunteth not itself, is not puffed up"
ambition	"doth not behave itself unseemly, seeketh not its own,"
frustration, rage, resentment, hatred	"is not provoked"

Love is the one and only antidote that can save man from the many diseases produced by the emotions of our evil nature. Psychiatrist Smiley Blanton emphasized this fact in the title of one of his books, *Love or Perish*. Without love—that thoughtfulness and keen consideration of others—man is likely to perish from a variety of diseases of mind and body.

An internationally known psychiatrist, Alfred Adler, writes, "The most important task imposed by religion has always been, 'Love thy neighbor. . . .' It is the individual who is not interested in his fellow man who has the greatest difficulties in life and provides the greatest injury to others. It is from among such individuals that all human failures spring."[2] Dr. Adler based these sweeping conclusions on a careful analysis of thousands of patients. He observed that a lack of love was observed in "all human failures."

This is in line with Biblical teaching. Love was the cornerstone of the Old Testament. Jesus did not disturb that stone but made it the cornerstone of the New Testament when he said, "Thou shalt love the Lord thy God with all thy heart, and with all thy soul, and with all thy mind. This is the great and first commandment. And a second like unto it is this, Thou shalt love thy neighbor as thyself. On these two commandments the whole law hangeth, and the prophets."[3]

When I quote the Bible and Dr. Adler to patients who are suffering physically and mentally from a lack of love, some of them retort that it is very difficult to change one's feelings—to change hate to love. That is true. Psychologists support this view, claiming that the will does not have complete control over the emotions. However, these psychologists also state that the will has good control over our actions. Our wills, therefore, largely do have the power to decide what we do and what we don't do. That is fortunate, because actions, over which we do have power, can change our feelings. Jesus said, "Love your enemies, bless them that curse you, do good to them that hate you. . . ."[4] Do something good for your enemy and it will surprise you to find how much easier it is to love him. This is the Scripturally and psychologically sound method of changing our feelings. It will work as many wonders as were ever ascribed to Aladdin's lamp.

"Do good to them that hate you." Impossible? Not if you follow some easy directions. The first step in the performance of the impossible is to walk out into your kitchen. Now, you *can* do that. You have done it many times and you can walk there again.

Step number two! Make up a lemon meringue pie as delicious as one on a magazine cover. Or make a pecan pie if that is your forte. Actually the kind isn't too important as long as you dress up that pie as though it were going on exhibition. You have made your pie. So far so good! By that time you will begin to feel a little better.

Give your feet the sternest look they ever got, and inform them in a tone of authority, "Feet, you are going to carry me and this pie to Mrs. Quirk's. Yes, I know you haven't been there in many a year, but you are going today."

Off you go. As you begin your adventure to seek the golden fleece of love, you feel strangely different. You feel warm, behind and a little to the left of your wishbone. You sense something wonderful happening inside. It gives you the same anticipation as the sight of icicles melting in the April sun.

Across the railroad tracks you go and down the dingy alley called Depot Street. You begin to understand Mrs. Quirk's attitude a little better as a heavy, noisy freight train passes, shaking houses and sidewalks, as the black soot soils your immaculate white gloves, and as dirty, boisterous children send shivers up your spine with their shrieks and cursing.

"Yes," you say to yourself, "if I had to live here, I think I would be irritable, too."

As you go up the steps, you cannot help smiling at the vastly new role you are playing. You rap on the door and wait. To Mrs. Quirk's truly surprised look, you present your peace offering with a nice smile that you decide to throw in for good measure.

A little chat in the living room, a cordial invitation for her to visit you, then on leaving a mutual hug and kiss—the fervor and spontaneity of it surprises both of you. You sense that a divine miracle has happened inside you because the love of God is truly coursing through your whole being. The impossible has happened! On your way home you feel like skipping along the street, as you did when you were a carefree girl. Inside is the spirit of singing and summer, absent for many a year.

You feel so well you decide you don't need to stop at the doctor's to take that "shot" for your frayed nerves. They aren't frayed any more. You never felt better in your life—even the pain in your back is gone.

> He drew a circle that shut me out—
> Heretic, rebel, a thing to flout.
> But Love and I had the wit to win:
> We drew a circle that took him in.[5]

"Love your enemies, do good to them that hate you." That may be a very bitter tonic to swallow but you will discover that when it reaches the heart, it will be surprisingly invigorating and exhilarating. You can love; you need not perish. By *doing* good you can change hate to love.

Obedience to the Lord in loving others, even the unlovely, will save you from a host of debilitating and serious diseases. Only when such love exists between individuals, between races, and between nations is there any hope for the world.

CHAPTER 14

Cats and Crocodiles

WHEN A CAT UNEXPECTEDLY ENCOUNTERS A DOG, THE hairs on the back of the cat stand on end. Its heart beats much faster, the blood pressure is raised, and breathing is accelerated. Adrenaline and other glandular products are immediately squirted into the blood stream because the emotional center, aroused by fear, sends lightning-quick messages of alarm to all parts of the body. The body's response to these messages is called the *alarm reaction*.

A close relative to the cat is the lion, which we have often seen in the zoo. In his cage he restlessly paces back and forth hundreds of times in a day. He is fearful, fidgety and frustrated. When he stops a moment to peer through the bars, his expression is anxious and there are deep vertical furrows in his forehead—the exact brow and image of a man who is making out his annual income tax return.

In another part of the zoo is the crocodile, quite a contrast to the lion. Mr. Crocodile lies there, motionless as an old log; rarely does he even blink an eye. He is the animalization of tranquility. He certainly doesn't worry about what the Lyons might say about him; neither is he trying to keep up with the Barrs. Bumps and blemishes on his face he has aplenty, but he has never shed any crocodile tears over them.

How long do these two different animals live? In one zoo I saw a lion that was twenty-five years old. His eyes were dim and his gait was unsteady. He was truly decrepit and sorely in need of dentures. At only twenty-five he was ready for the boneyard.

Is the crocodile old at twenty-five? Not at all! He lives long after the bones of the lion are dried and bleached.

Why are these two animals so vastly different in their

life spans? Dr. George Crile gave a group of doctors the answer in his Cleveland Clinic Museum. He had mounted many stuffed animals from all over the world, and by the side of each animal were exact replicas of its adrenal and thyroid glands.

The lion had very large adrenal glands. He had lived a life of great stress and alarm reactions were frequent occurrences. The lion's emotional center was ever calling for plenty of adrenaline for his long hard flights after swift antelope or fierce fights with other lions and African buffaloes. The lion had a large thyroid gland, indicating that he had packed the hours with strenuous activity.

In marked contrast these same glands in the crocodile were very small. His emotional center had not been making rapid demands for their products, and adrenaline had not repeatedly whipped his heart to full-throttle speed. Nor had adrenaline been raising the blood pressure and prematurely hardening the arteries.

In a human being the number of alarms sent out from the emotional center determines the size of stress glands such as the adrenal and thyroid. The New York State Department of Health published photographs of two human adrenal glands. One gland was normal in size, the other hypertrophied and greatly enlarged, "a result of stress."[1] The individual from whom the enlarged gland was removed probably died many years ahead of his time because the increased supply of adrenaline played havoc with one or more of his bodily functions. He not only shortened his days, but his days were likely filled with emotional turmoil.

One also must remember that the adrenal and thyroid glands are normally beneficial and necessary. If one awakes at night to the fact that a burglar is in the house, fear arouses the emotional center to send out messages to these glands for an increased supply of their hormones to enable the individual's heart to beat faster and to give him more energy for either a fight or a flight. This reserve of energy made available by the glands can be lifesaving if one is running from a lion or crossing a busy highway.

However, if a person sits at high noon in the security of his own home and allows his mind to think of burglars and charging bulls, his emotional center will send out identical alarm messages to the glands, heart and blood-pressure centers, as it would if the individual were actually attacked. Although the body needs an excess of hormones for genuine emergency situations, an excessive and frequent production of hormones over weeks and months results in deleterious responses.

The stresses of living are not nearly as responsible for a host of debilitating diseases as are our faulty reactions to those stresses. The office of a physician is filled with people suffering from nearly every disease in the book because their minds are beset by a thousand worries about their finances, their health or their children.

Sometimes it is the doctor who suffers. Recently I was faced with a loss of some money. The loss was on my mind when I went to bed and it awakened me about 4 A.M. The next night I didn't sleep well because I was

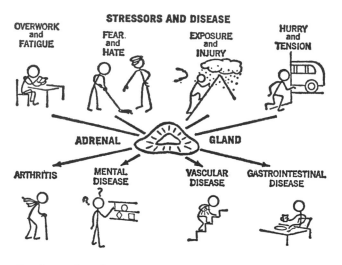

Based on a chart that appeared in *New York State Health News,* February, 1955.

depressed. I am sure my adrenal and other glands were pumping an excess of deleterious hormones into my system. I think my worrying would have continued for a long time, but on the second morning I had immediate relief from my depressed feelings when I began to practice this verse from the Bible: "Be thankful, whatever the circumstances may be."[2] Before I read that verse I was the victim of circumstances; afterwards I was the master of them.

I experienced far more relief than I would have gained from a sedative or a tranquilizer, which can give no inner peace and only temporarily blocks some of the impulses going out from the emotional center. Much more helpful and permanent is another prescription from the Book of books: "Don't worry over anything whatever; tell God every detail of your needs in earnest and thankful prayer, and the peace of God, which transcends human understanding, will keep constant guard over your hearts and minds as they rest in Christ Jesus."[3]

I know some words that are a prescription worth a thousand dollars, and I have prescribed them many times to sick men and women. Actually they are worth far more to anyone who memorizes them and determines that they shall be the standard of what he thinks and talks about: "Finally, brethren, whatsoever things are true, whatsoever things are honest, whatsoever things are just, whatsoever things are pure, whatsoever things are lovely, whatsoever things are of good report; if there be any virtue, and if there be any praise, think on these things."[4]

CHAPTER 15

You're As Old As Your Arteries

IN RUNNING LIFE'S GAUNTLET OF MANY KILLERS, THE runner is offered much help by medical science. He can now get safely past Mr. Diabetes by blinding him with a few squirts of insulin. Often Mr. Cancer can be eliminated by the talents of a surgeon. Even Mr. Pneumonia can now be liquidated by shooting him with penicillin.

But along that line, successfully defying medical weapons and wielding a bigger cutlass with every passing year, stands Mr. Arteriosclerosis. In fact, recent statistics reveal that this one savage alone scalps fifty-four per cent of all gauntlet runners.[1]

One can understand how diseased arteries are responsible for so many deaths when he knows that bad arteries are the basic cause of strokes of apoplexy, of coronary heart attacks, of angina pectoris, of gangrene of the bowel and legs, of certain kidney diseases, as well as other fatal conditions. Arteries cause widespread trouble because their openings become clogged and the blood clots in them. Since living tissue requires blood, dire results and death follow quickly when the body's blood supply is cut off. If the arteries to the vital organs of the body could only be kept open, half of the people who now die would go on living.

Truly a man is as old as his arteries. Arteriosclerosis has properly been called "Everybody's Disease."

What can we do to dodge man's most savage killer? Medical literature abounds with studies showing the importance of reducing a fatty substance called cholesterol. Cholesterol tumors form in the walls of blood vessels and obstruct the openings of the arteries. These tumors are called *atheromas,* hence the term *atherosclerosis* for the most important type of arteriosclerosis.

At this writing great emphasis is being placed on reducing cholesterol in the blood, since there appears to be a close connection between high levels of cholesterol and atherosclerosis. Many recent scientific studies show that the important agents that increase this dangerous cholesterol in the blood are:

1. Eating fat of animals
2. Overweight
3. Smoking
4. Carnal emotions and stress.

In the past few years medical science has awakened to the fact that the eating of animal fat is an important cause of arteriosclerosis. This fat forms the tiny, fatty, cholesterol tumors within the walls of the arteries, which hinder the flow of blood. Now, in this decade, magazines, radio and TV are broadcasting the good news that we can reduce the ravages from man's greatest killer by cutting down our intake of animal fats. Happy as we are with the fact that medical science has arrived, we may be amazed to discover that our ultramodern research is about thirty-five hundred years behind the Book of books:

"And the Lord spake unto Moses, saying, Speak unto the children of Israel, saying, Ye shall eat no manner of fat, of ox, or of sheep, or of goat. And the fat of the beast . . . may be used in any other use: But ye shall in no wise eat of it."[2] Because the Lord wanted to emphasize the tremendous danger of arteriosclerosis, He repeated his previous admonition not to eat animal fat.[3]

Overweight is another important factor in the

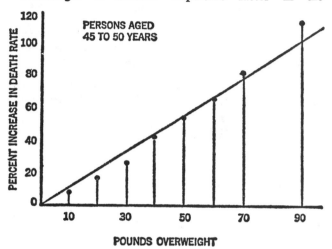

Pounds overweight	Increase in death rate over average, %
10	8
20	18
30	28
40	45
50	56
60	67
70	81
90	116

formation of cholesterol plaques within the arteries. Since overweight is composed of fat, the obese already have plenty of animal fat under their own skins. In a recent textbook we read: "It is no new doctrine that gluttons have a relatively high morbidity and mortality from vascular disease. . . . More recent evidence has strengthened this traditional impression. It is stated with statistical support that the obese have a greater incidence of hypertension (high blood pressure) and that atherosclerotic plaques develop earlier and more abundantly in the over-fed."[4]

Centuries before, the inspired Apostle Paul wrote to Titus who was preaching in Crete: "A prophet from their own people said of them, Cretans are . . . lazy gluttons. This testmony is true. For this reason correct them sternly, so they may be sound in the faith. . . ."[5]

The Bible has many other references, direct and in-direct, which warn against intemperance in eating. Obe-dience to the warnings would make for efficiency, pleasant appearance, character building, happiness and longevity.

Smoking also increases the cholesterol in the blood. This fact could well explain why, in a study of 187,000 men over a period of forty-four months, it was discovered that one third of the coronary deaths were attributable to smoking.[6] The United States' vital statistics for 1957 revealed that arteriosclerotic heart disease killed 452,507 people, and one can assume that smoking alone was re-sponsible for about 150,000 of these unfortunate deaths.[7]

How can smoking increase cholesterol in the blood? Philadelphia researchers have recently shown that it is the nicotine which results in the formation of the following substances, in this order: adrenaline, free fatty acids, and cholesterol. They report that both smoking and psychic stress produce adrenaline, and adrenaline calls forth from the fatty deposits of the body the slow but sure killer—cholesterol.[8] Since both smoking and psychic stress can produce adrenaline, which in turn produces cholesterol, we can now understand even the method by which smok-ing and psychic stress kill human beings.

Now a further word about psychic stress. Although medical science now knows the chemicals stress releases in the body to produce its lethal effects, medical science can offer little help to prevent stress and fear from affect-ing people.

Political science boldly asserted in 1941 that it would eliminate man's mighty enemy—fear. Former president Franklin D. Roosevelt met with the great leaders of the world and incorporated in the Atlantic Charter the Four Freedoms. This Charter bid fair to be included among the greatest doctrines of all ages because it promised to all nations Four Freedoms, one of them being freedom from fear.

Four short years after this promise of millennial blessedness, the first atomic bomb was dropped, killing thousands and subjecting tens of thousands to excruciating suffering and lingering death. Realizing that women, children and the aged were as vulnerable as the soldier in the front line trench, the world was filled with immeasurable fear such as had never before gripped mankind. H. G. Wells, reflecting the fear of that day, said, "This world is at the end of its tether. The end of everything we call life is at hand."[9]

In the years since that first devastating bomb was dropped, far mightier bombs have been developed. Stress and the diseases from fear are increasing. One authority has said there is only one chance out of five that the world would finish this century without far-reaching devastation.

Speaking before the United Nations on September 26, 1961, President John F. Kennedy said, "Every man, woman and child lives under a nuclear sword of Damocles, hanging by the slenderest of threads, capable of being cut at any moment by accident, miscalculation, or madness."

One Book offers freedom from the fear and stress of this atomic age. One Book can make the statement with confidence because it has proved its value to millions subjected to all types of fears. The Book of books abounds in assurances that have comforted and helped men and women in every walk of life:

Surely he shall deliver thee from the snare of the fowler,
    and from the noisome pestilence.
He shall cover thee with his feathers,
    and under his wings shalt thou trust. . . .
Thou shalt not be afraid for the terror by night;
    nor for the arrow that flieth by day;
Nor for the pestilence that walketh in darkness;
    nor for the destruction that wasteth at noonday.
A thousand shall fall at thy side, and
    ten thousand at thy right hand;
    but it shall not come nigh thee.[10]

Scoffers will retort, "Don't you know the atomic bombs are so powerful now that one of them blew a small Pacific island out of the sea?" Perhaps the Lord had the inspired writer record Psalm 46 for us in this atomic day:

God is our refuge and strength,
  a very present help in trouble.
  therefore will not we fear,
Though the earth be removed,
  and though the mountains be carried into the midst
  of the sea;
Though the waters thereof roar and be troubled,
  though the mountains shake with the swelling thereof.[11]

Be still, and know that I am God;
I will be exalted among the nations,
I will be exalted in the earth.
Jehovah of hosts is with us;
The God of Jacob is our refuge.[12]

Today the world outlook is darker than at any previous
time in history. Yet to the believing Christian the gloom
is only an indication of the imminent and glorious return
of Jesus Christ. The believer need not entertain fear. As
times grow worse, he has more reason to look up, for
his deliverance is close at hand.

CHAPTER 16

David and the Giant—Worry

"DOCTOR, I CAME TO YOU BECAUSE I AM ALL TUCKERED
out. Before this thing hit me I could work all day and
not be tired. Now, when I start across the field on the
tractor, I get so weak that I stop before I get halfway
across. I have to get off the tractor and lie down by the
fence before I get strength to go on. That's not like me.
For the past month I have been completely bushed. I
have been losing weight, too."

I stared in amazement at a husky, twenty-year-old
farmer. He was the type who was never sick, yet here he
was wholly incapacited for work. My first thoughts were
of severe anemia, leukemia, or perhaps internal bleeding.

The possibility of cancer and tuberculosis came to my mind. However, a physical examination and laboratory tests showed no organic trouble.

I questioned the young man more carefully. I discovered that his attractive fianceé was doing a little dating with another lad. Also, a man who had promised to give him a good bargain on a used car had now raised the price two hundred dollars. The fear of losing both girl and car had been causing my patient to lose his appetite, his sleep and his strength.

Yes, this unusual fatigue was entirely due to worry and anxiety. Dr. Hans Selye, a world authority on stress, has shown that long and continued stress results in exhaustion. Not work but worry makes us weary. Explaining the situation to my patient and giving him a few sedative tablets did the trick. His normal strength came back and even his appearance improved so much that he won and married the girl of his choice.

Perhaps you have had a similar experience. Some days you work hard from early morning until late at night without experiencing fatigue. Then, another day, you are frayed out by the middle of the day. The next time you have such unusual weariness, pause and think. Often you will be able to remember some emotional upset. It may not be anything more than the boss looking over your sales record and asking, "Is that the best you can do?" Or you may have worn a new dress, one you made yourself, and not a single person in the office made a comment about it.

Patients often tell me that they are just as tired upon arising as when they went to bed. Sleep refreshes our exhaustion from work, but not the weariness that stems from worry. Far too many people take their anxieties to bed with them. The best medicine for that is to count one's blessings and thank the Lord for His gifts and kindnesses.

Anxiety can manifest itself in other ways. A mother brought to me her five-year-old son, who was plastered with hives. She inquired, "Doctor, what causes my Tony to break out like this? He never had hives until the past few months. His diet has not changed."

She hesitated. When I urged her to continue, she laughed and said, "You may think I am foolish, but Tony gets hives only when he stays all day with his aunt. She moved here recently, and keeping her house spic and span has always been her god. It is true Tony is a careless youngster, but his aunt scolds and nags him constantly. Fear of her couldn't possibly—?"

"Oh, yes," I replied. "Not infrequently hives are caused by an emotional upset." I advised her to park Tony elsewhere. He has never had another attack of hives.

Then there was Mrs. Shirley Johnson, who would come into my office with one or both eyes nearly swollen shut. Her lips were swollen to three times their size. She had experienced angioneurotic edema so often that she recognized the cause: emotional stress, such as the fear of driving in city traffic or the fear and bustle of entertaining many people. The name of this condition, angio*neurotic* edema, indicates its association with stress.

Asthma can also be triggered by stress. The difficult breathing of asthma induces fear and tension which aggravate the condition a great deal by establishing a vicious circle.

A psychiatrist told of a patient who developed asthma every time he heard a church bell ring. The cause of these onsets is intriguing. His trouble began several years before, while he was waiting for his bride to arrive at the church. As the church bell was ringing, a messenger arrived with the news that his fiancée had changed her mind, and the emotional shock induced a severe attack of asthma in the man. In the years that followed, every time he heard a church bell he was seized with an attack of asthma.

The Psalmist David had more reasons than most of us to have justifiable fears. Consider his encounters with a lion, a bear, the giant Goliath, and the many times he missed death at the hands of King Saul. David saved himself from a host of psychosomatic diseases because he always put his trust in the Lord: "The Lord is my light and my salvation; whom shall I fear? The Lord is the stronghold of my life; of whom shall I be afraid? . . . Though an army should encamp against me, my heart shall not fear: though war should rise against me, I would still be confident."[1]

High blood pressure can be caused not only by hates, as previously shown, but also by worries. For this reason physicians seek to keep their patients from knowing what the pressure is when it has gone up. That knowledge could induce fear and shoot the pressure still higher, with serious results. One authority advises physicians in such cases to do "a little judicious lying," because he considers a lie a justifiable portion of some therapeutic programs: "This maneuver [lying] may effectively prevent the patient from developing an anxiety neurosis and 'heart consciousness.' It has been our belief and experience that most of the subjective symptoms associated with essential hypertension [high blood pressure] are psychogenically [emotionally] induced."[2]

This quotation demonstrates the importance of the giant Worry in causing and aggravating high blood pressure, and the great lengths that physicians are willing to go to save their patients. However, lying as always creates more problems than it solves, and sooner or later the patient will discover the truth. Then the physician has lost his most important bond with his patient—confidence.

All of us have had and will continue to have encounters with the giant Worry, and it will be helpful to recall a bit of history. When the mighty King Saul and his forces were cowering in the face of the giant Goliath, the stripling David was stirred by Israel's lack of faith in God. Refusing the accepted methods of fighting giants, David went out armed with a mighty faith in God and a sanctified slingshot. Was he afraid? "In the day when I am afraid, I will have confidence in Thee. In God, I will praise His word; in God I trust, I will not fear; what can flesh do to me?"[3]

David's faith was bound to conquer and it did. In our everyday encounters with big and little worries, the practice of our faith decides whether we cower or conquer. David was able to conquer not only Goliath but also worry on many occasions. Perhaps that is one reason why his psalms are so helpful in dealing with worry.

To those who are dubious about the ability of God's Word and His Spirit to help men with modern problems, Dr. Howard Kelly has written something pertinent: "I testify that the Bible is the Word of God because it is food for the spirit just as definitely as bread and meat are food for the body. The Bible appeals strongly to me as a physician, because it is such excellent medicine; it has never yet failed to cure a single patient if only he took his prescription."[4]

No prescription has ever helped more people than the Twenty-third Psalm. It can be taken with meals and before retiring and as often as needed. It will give a man energy to be more than a conqueror over the giant Worry and his bag of diseases:

> The Lord is my shepherd: I shall
> not want.
> He maketh me to lie down in green pastures:
> He leadeth me beside the still waters.
> He restoreth my soul: he leadeth me in the
> paths of righteousness for his name's sake.
> Yea, though I walk through the valley of the
> shadow of death, I will fear no evil: for thou
> art with me, thy rod and thy staff they
> comfort me.[5]

CHAPTER 17

Arthritis From a Panther Scare

A FARMER ABOUT FORTY-FIVE YEARS OF AGE CAME INTO MY office some time ago to consult me about an abdominal complaint. I observed that his fingers on both hands were badly deformed with rheumatoid arthritis and I asked, "How long have you had this arthritis?"

"Ever since I was a little fellow about nine years old," he replied. "You see there was a panther scare in the neighborhood at that time. In going and returning from school, I had to pass through a stretch of woods, and every time I ran through the woods, I was scared stiff thinking the panther might leap on me. After a couple of weeks my hands began to look this way. They have been deformed ever since."

The development of arthritis from fear and other emotional disturbances is common. We do not understand the mechanism, but the fact of its occurrence is well known. Some people who are crippled for life in many of their joints give a clear-cut history of emotional stress. After the disease becomes established, flare-ups and spreading of the arthritis follow emotional crises and prolonged tensions. Stresses such as breaking an engagement, getting a divorce, having financial tangles, harboring resentments, or losing a loved one, are only a few of the causative agents.

Of course, arthritis can also be caused by fatigue, injury or exposure to wet and cold, which are also properly considered stress factors. Arthritis victims number two million sufferers in the United States alone.

Many a man fears he is going to lose an acre of his farm or even a few inches of a city lot because of the claims of his neighbor. Surveyors give conflicting opinions. Foolish and impractical seem the words of Jesus to a man in this situation: ". . . if any man will sue thee at the law, and take away thy coat, let him have thy cloak also."[1] The disturbed man considers His advice idealistic and ill suited to a twentieth-century problem. Instead, he decides to fight it out in the courts and hires a lawyer.

During the long months before his case is called, and during the tense days of the trial and the months after the trial, his pituitary gland, his adrenals and his thyroid glands work overtime to pump their products into his system. When the judge hands down the decision, the contesting neighbor takes the man's shirt, his lawyer takes his coat, and the court costs take his trousers. All too often such a man ends up in a wheel chair for the rest of his life with a disabling arthritis—a high price to pay for refusing the Lord's advice.

Any discussion of the effect of fear on the body would not be complete without considering the effect of this emotion on the heart. I recall the case of a prominent Israeli physician who was reading a newspaper account of the murderous persecution of Jews in Russia, where many of his relatives lived. To a friend in the room, he mentioned the great fear he felt for the safety of his loved ones. A moment later he slumped over dead in his chair, a victim of a clot of the coronary artery (the artery that supplies the heart with blood).

Can fear really precipitate clotting of blood such as occurs in that most common heart killer—coronary thrombosis? Dr. David Macht gave the answer at the 1951 annual meeting of the American Medical Association in Atlantic City. In his laboratory he had measured the number of

minutes required for the blood of fifty normally happy
people to clot, and he compared this clotting time with the
clotting time of the blood of a hundred nervous people.
Here is a tabulation of his results:

	Clotting Time
50 normally happy people	8 — 12 minutes
50 apprehensive people	4 — 5 minutes
50 highly nervous people	1 — 3 minutes

Dr. Macht concluded, "It was surprising to find that
such a profound influence was produced by ordinary acute
and transient emotions in healthy persons."[2]

A previous chapter revealed that when arteries become
partially obstructed by tiny cholesterol plaques, the flow
of blood is slowed and the blood is more likely to form a
clot, which completely stops the circulation. Dr. Macht
showed that stress is another very important factor in
causing blood to clot.

In other words, stress not only narrows the artery and
greatly slows the blood flow to facilitate clotting, but it
also affects the blood itself so that it is much more likely
to clot. Hence, we see the almost unbelievable importance
of stress in both setting the stage for and performing the
act of clotting. A number of recent medical articles have
emphasized the importance of stress in this condition.[8]
However, we must not paint a lopsided picture of the
importance of stress by ignoring the other factors that play
a part in setting the stage for clotting, such as eating
animal fat, overeating and smoking.

Dr. Hans Selye's definition of stress embraces not only
the emotions of hate, fear and sorrow, but also includes
external factors such as cold, light and noise. Many an
individual who has set the stage for a fatal heart attack
by overeating fatty and other foods, or smoking, or worrying, actually succumbs when he walks against a cold wind
or goes out to shovel snow.

Consider the stress that my wife once experienced on
our Canadian fishing trip. My wife, daughter and I arrived
at Matawan, Ontario, about five o'clock on a Saturday
evening. We had to catch some fish for our Sunday meals,
so my daughter Linda and I rowed a boat up the treacher-
ous Matawan Rapids, which was new territory to us. My
wife stayed in the cabin to unpack and arrange things for
the night. Then she sat down to await our return. Eight
o'clock came, but no boat came down the swiftly moving

river. Then nine o'clock, nine-thirty—still no daughter, no husband, appeared.

If my wife had become excited or hysterical, she might have developed a number of medical conditions. But the Lord reminded her of a verse in Psalm 34 which we had been memorizing on our vacation: "I sought the Lord, and he heard me, and delivered me from all my fears."[4] My wife sought the Lord and He gave her remarkable deliverance from all her fears as she sat alone on the dock in the darkness, the lantern by her side.

At ten o'clock she heard the voice of Linda behind her on the shore: "Daddy sent me by land, because he did not want to bring me down the rapids in the dark. The fish were slow in biting, but once they started they bit like a house afire!"

Still more waiting. Ten-thirty, and no boat. To my wife's calls no answer came from the dark, swirling river. She knew she was doing everything feasible by keeping the lantern on the dock. She had ample reason to fear, but the Lord gave her that peace of mind that passeth understanding. She did not panic or start off with the lantern to search for help. Instead, her faith in the Scriptural promise that the Lord had tailored for this special need gave her restful assurance. Divine strength she needed, since it was not until eleven o'clock that the evidence of her faith arrived safely at the dock.

CHAPTER 18

Cutting Man's Greatest Fear
Down to Size

NEARLY EVERYBODY HAS BEEN IN A J. C. PENNEY STORE, one of the world's largest chains of drygoods stores, with seventeen hundred branches in the United States. But few people know about one of the most important events in the life of J. C. Penney, the founder.

In the crash of 1929, J. C. Penney's business was solid but he had made some unwise personal commitments. He became so worried that he couldn't sleep. Then he developed "shingles," a disorder that can cause great annoyance and severe pain. He was hospitalized and given sedatives, but got no relief and tossed all night. A combination of circumstances had broken him so completely, physically and mentally, that he was overwhelmed with a fear of death. He wrote farewell letters to his wife and son, for he did not expect to live until morning.

The next morning the great business tycoon heard singing in the hospital chapel. He pulled himself together and entered as the group was singing "God Will Take Care of You." Then followed a Scripture reading and a prayer. In Mr. Penney's own words, "Suddenly something happened. I can't explain it. I can only call it a miracle. I felt as if I had been instantly lifted out of the darkness of a dungeon into warm, brilliant sunlight. I felt as if I had been transported from hell to paradise. I felt the power of God as I had never felt it before. I realized then that I alone was responsible for all my troubles. I know that God with His love was there to help me. From that day to this, my life has been free from worry. I am seventy-one years old, and the most dramatic and glorious minutes of my life were those I spent in that chapel that morning: 'God Will Take Care of You.' "[1]

Thus, a man has been able to dwarf every fear because he saw a loving, heavenly Father—his Father—anxious and ready to take care of him in life's dilemmas.

William Ewart Gladstone, on being questioned for the secret of the unusual serenity he was able to maintain in spite of situational stresses, replied, "At the foot of my bed, where I can see it on retiring and on arising in the morning, are the words, 'Thou wilt keep him in perfect peace, whose mind is stayed on thee: because he trusteth in thee.' "[2]

Some psychiatrists have given far more than superficial help in the medical textbooks they have written for physicians. William Sadler advises physicians how to get at the cause of people's troubles:

Prayer is a powerful and effectual worry-remover. Men and women who have learned to pray with childlike sincerity, literally talking to, and communicating with the Heavenly Father, are in possession of the great secret whereby they can cast their care upon God, knowing that He careth for us. A clear conscience is a great step toward barricading the mind against neuroticism.

Many are victims of fear and worry because they fail properly to maintain their spiritual nutrition. . . . The majority of people liberally feed their bodies, and many make generous provision for their mental nourishment; but the vast majority leave the soul to starve, paying very little attention to their spiritual nutrition; and as a result the spiritual nature is so weakened that it is unable to exercise the restraining influence over the mind which would enable it to surmount its difficulties and maintain an atmosphere above conflict and despondency.[8]

He further advises physicians to encourage their patients to engage "in daily, systematic Bible reading." In fact, in his textbook for doctors, Dr. Sadler prints forty-three different verses as examples of the therapeutic value of Bible reading. We shall give only eight of them here. Each of them, if assimilated into the mind, can accomplish more than any sedative or tranquilizer:

If we confess our sins, he is faithful and just to forgive us our sins, and to cleanse us from all unrighteousness (I John 1:9, KJV).

Come unto me, all ye that labour and are heavy laden, and I will give you rest. Take my yoke upon you, and learn of me; for I am meek and lowly in heart: and ye shall find rest unto your souls (Matthew 11:28-29, KJV).

Behold, I stand at the door, and knock: if any man hear my voice, and open the door, I will come in to him, and will sup with him, and he with me (Revelation 3:20, KJV).

Create in me a clean heart, O God; and renew a right spirit within me (Psalm 51:10, KJV).

Peace I leave with you, my peace I give unto you: not as the world giveth, give I unto you. Let not your heart be troubled, neither let it be afraid (John 14:27, KJV).

Behold, God is my salvation; I will trust, and not be afraid: for the Lord Jehovah is my strength and my song; he also is become my salvation (Isaiah 12:2, KJV).

But my God shall supply all your need according to his riches in glory by Christ Jesus (Philippians 4:19, KJV).

I can do all things through Christ which strengtheneth me (Philippians 4:13, KJV).

For he shall give his angels charge over thee, to keep thee in all thy ways. They shall bear thee up in their hands, lest thou dash thy foot against a stone (Psalm 91:11-12, KJV).

These verses become alive and real only after we have experienced them. The night I asked God, for Christ's sake, to forgive my sins, I was weighed down with a sense of guilt and fear. After a few moments of confession and forsaking of sin, the guilt and fears vanished, and a miraculous, heaven-sent joy filled my mind. Instead of long-continued and expensive trips to a psychiatrist's couch to get rid of a disease-producing *guilt complex,* I made one trip to God's altar and got rid of *guilt itself.*

The Bible says that God removes the guilt "As far as the east is from the west. . . ."[4] From that moment I felt very grateful to God, and love sprang up between us. I experienced what John wrote: "There is no fear in love; but perfect love casteth out fear. . . ."[5] As love increases, fear decreases.

Last summer as I sat in the yard, a chipmunk approached

a hole in the ground only three feet away from me. His cheeks were ballooned with food for his loved ones down in the hole. Because I was so very close, he hesitated, but not for long. His love for the young ones overcame his fear and into the hole he skipped.

Love for Christ and His Word helped Jim Vaus when he needed relief from fear. Before his conversion, Jim had been the wiretapper for the infamous underworld gang of Mickey Cohen in Los Angeles. The morning after his conversion during a Billy Graham meeting, the newspapers blazoned the story about him.

When Jim Vaus read the morning papers, he began to do some serious thinking. What action would the gangsters take about this matter? After all, Jim knew a host of secrets that might send some of the gang to the penitentiary, if not to the gas chamber. From the gang's viewpoint, Jim's conversion meant he had turned traitor to them, and he knew that a desertion with gang secrets called for speedy liquidation.

When he put down the paper, he didn't have long to wait. As he looked out the window, a big limousine stopped in front of his house. Jim recognized the men who emerged as some of the most heartless killers in the underworld. Looking carefully up and down the street, they approached his front door. Did Jim become panicky and make for the back door?

If ever a man had reason to run in fear for his life, he did. If he had been in such danger twenty-four hours earlier, he certainly would have fled—and probably would still be running. But he didn't run, because the love of God filled his being and strengthened him with a verse the Lord had given him that morning when he opened his Bible at random: "When a man's ways please the Lord, he maketh even his enemies to be at peace with him."[6]

Jim opened the door to the gunmen and they told him that a wiretapping job had been assigned to him. He must fly to St. Louis immediately, or else. Jim told them he couldn't go because the Lord had changed his heart. When he described his conversion, his visitors looked bewildered and left. Jim knew that the Lord had fulfilled the verse He had given him.

The "dread of death" is undoubtedly man's greatest fear. However, millions of men and women have gone through the valley of the shadow of death without any apprehension. John Bunyan expressed the attitude of many Christians when he wrote: "Let dissolution come when it will, it can do the Christian no harm, for it be but a passage out of a prison into a palace; out of a sea of troubles into a haven of rest; out of a crowd of enemies, to an innumerable company of true, loving, and faithful friends; out of shame, reproach, and contempt into exceeding great and eternal glory."

The Apostle Paul was able to dwarf the greatest fear of all when he looked death in the face and exultingly exclaimed, "So when this corruptible shall have put on incorruption, and this mortal shall have put on immortality, then shall be brought to pass the saying that is written, Death is swallowed up in victory. O death, where is thy sting? O grave, where is thy victory?"[7]

Truly, in every age the Spirit and Word of God have provided abundant deliverance for Christians from fears and their long trains of diseases. Even the master of all fears, *death,* should hold no terror for the believer who has his eyes on the resurrection and eternal joyful life. Only the Christian is able to heed the advice of William Cullen Bryant:

> So live, that when thy summons comes to join
> The innumerable caravan which moves
> To that mysterious realm, where each shall take
> His chamber in the silent halls of death,
> Thou go not, like the quarry-slave at night,
> Scourged to his dungeon, but, sustained and soothed
> By an unfaltering trust, approach thy grave,
> Like one that wraps the drapery of his couch
> About him, and lies down to pleasant dreams.[8]

CHAPTER 19

"See Farther Through a Tear Than Through a Telescope"

LATE ONE AFTERNOON A HEALTHY YOUNG MARRIED WOMAN received the shocking news that her husband had been instantly killed. Any of us can sympathize with her in the grief, heartache and tears that she experienced during the evening and long hours of the night when she couldn't sleep. The one who meant everything to her had been cruelly snatched away. She was so completely and irreconcilably overwhelmed with grief that she refused to listen to anything her sympathetic friends tried to say.

If chemical tests could have been made of her blood, they would have disclosed the presence of a great increase in hormones and abnormal toxins from the pituitary, thyroid and adrenal glands. That somethng was present in toxic amounts is proved by the fact that the next morning some of her fingers and her wrist joints were stiff, swollen and painful. This was the onset of an arthritis that eventually invalided the young woman.

Thus we see that not only the emotions of hate and fear are capable of causing a variety of serious and fatal diseases. The emotion of sorrow can also damage the body. Grief can trigger onsets of ulcerative colitis, rheumatoid arthritis, asthma, and many other diseases.

To prevent the minor and major diseases resulting from the inundating grief over a loved one's death, the Bible provides the greatest possible barricade. The eleventh chapter of John not only gives clear teaching on this matter but also presents public and highly dramatic proof of the veracity of the assertions made. In the village of Bethany lived Lazarus and his two sisters, Mary and Martha. When Lazarus became sick, word was sent to Jesus for help. But Jesus purposely delayed His going because He wanted to teach the world the transitory character of the state we call death. When Jesus started His trip to Bethany, He told His disciples that He was going to raise Lazarus out of his *sleep*.

The disciples thought it was rather ridiculous to make a hazardous journey to wake a sick man out of sleep. Then Jesus talked to them in the only language that they in their immaturity could understand: "Lazarus is dead."

Arriving in Bethany, Jesus revealed to a sister mourning for her dead brother another important aspect of the state that we erroneously call *death:* ". . . the believer in Me will live even when he dies, and everyone who lives and believes in Me shall never, never die. Do you believe this?"[1]

How could anybody believe that Christians never really die—that they are only asleep? Jesus knew that even His disciples and the others at Bethany would not believe such assertions without proof. A million empty human words never would have convinced anybody, but three words from the Master did: "Lazarus, come forth." Out came Lazarus, a living proof that for the Christians there is no horrible existence that we associate with the word *death*. It is only a sleep that requires His call to awaken us. Quite understandably, Christians changed the names of their graveyards to sleeping chambers (our English word "cemetery" comes from the Greek *koimeterion,* which means "a sleeping chamber").

When Jesus told those who were mourning over the dead body of Jairus' daughter, ". . . she is not dead, but sleepeth,"[2] they ridiculed Him with scornful epithets. Again He wanted to prove false the utterly hopeless view we have about the state we call *death*. So He merely took the cold and motionless girl by the hand and awakened her from the state that He calls *sleep*.

The Apostle Paul understood fully this new concept that Jesus had drilled into His disciples. In I Corinthians 15, Paul elaborates on this matter to show that all who have fallen asleep will be awakened by the trumpet call of the Master on His return to the earth. Paul also wrote to Christians in another church who had suffered the temporary loss of loved ones: "But we do not want to keep you in ignorance, brothers, about those who have fallen asleep, so you may not grieve as others do, who have no hope."[3]

Neither should we grieve today over our children and loved ones who are asleep in their chambers. Of course, we can be excused if we shed some tears over the separation. But Christians who truly believe what Jesus proved about the promise of their awakening should certainly not grieve with such bitter and tumultuous emotion that they bring down upon themselves arthritis and other diseases that the Bible enables them to avoid. It is both a wonderful privilege and a duty for believers to refrain from harboring despair and disease-producing grief when we know that our loved ones, though absent from our immediate presence, are sleeping.

One writer has expressed this temporary separation in another way: "I love to think of my little children whom God has called to Himself as away at school—at the best school in the universe, under the best teachers, learning the best things, in the best possible way."

Some may wonder why God allows His children to experience sorrow at all. Death is not a gift from God but a result of the sin of Adam—". . . death came through a man. . . ."[4] Throughout this book we have repeatedly seen that disease and death are products of sin; we can't blame God for them. Instead, we ought to give God the credit for our deliverance from the tragedy of death: "For just as in Adam all die, so in Christ shall all be made to live."[5] God is not the author of death, but the Giver of eternal life.

Not only in the future, but here in this life and now, the divine Alchemist can miraculously change a sorrowing heart of lead into a golden mellowness that sings praises through tears. A poet said, "Sorrows are our best educators. A man can see farther through a tear than through a telescope."

Is it not remarkable that the sorrows that cause devastating diseases in some people can in others develop character and maturity? Polishing is certainly not a pleasant process for the object being polished but it is a necessary procedure for every stone that becomes a gem. We admire the finished product, but we shrink from the process.

In December 1961, a letter brought sorrow to our home. For over three weeks we had not heard from our daughter who, with her husband, was engaged in missionary work in Southern Rhodesia. Then came a letter from her, written in a hospital where she had been a patient for several weeks. An examination of her spinal fluid revealed an abundance of a deadly fungus, Monilia. The well-trained English physicians had started her on a medication, but only as a gesture, for they were well aware that it had proved utterly worthless in cases of meningitic infection. They were reluctant to use a new and toxic drug because of its serious side effects.

This news from our only child, nine thousand miles away and stricken with a seemingly hopeless cerebrospinal infection, brought keen sorrow to my wife and me. Never before could we fully appreciate and sympathize with those who had lost their children.

Our grief might well have overwhelmed us if it had not been for the comfort and solace of God's Holy Spirit and the Bible. We wondered how people without Christ in their hearts were able to stand up under great sorrow. A thousand times more effective than any tranquilizer, the Lord gave us this Scriptural wonder drug: "For this slight, momentary trouble is producing for us an everlasting weight of glory that exceeds all calculations, granted we do not fasten our eyes on the visible but on the unseen; for the visible things are transitory, but the unseen things are everlasting."[6]

I saw that my crushing load of sorrow need not result in disease. Instead, it could give me "an everlasting weight of glory that exceeds all calculations. . . ." My attitude could determine whether my grief would cause a disease in me or a glorious and everlasting reward. It was my privilege to look through my tears and see farther than through any telescope to the glory of eternal verities.

Observe the condition: ". . . granted we do not fasten our eyes on the visible but on the unseen. . . ." An unreasonable condition? After all, if the Christian truly has the proper sense of proportion between the transitory things of this life, as compared to the eternal value of the life beyond, is it not a confession of doubt for him to mourn *unduly* for the passing of a loved one? Should the visible things and people of this earth assume greater value than eternal issues? Sorrow causes diseases in us because we *grieve over the past*. The Bible erases irreconcilable grief and prevents disease by telling us to *look forward to the future*.

In the weeks that followed the receipt of our daughter's first letter, the Word of God and His Spirit made life bearable for us. We had peace of mind because we had committed everything to Him.

My daughter, her husband, and their two babies were

flown home, and she was studied thoroughly in a Philadelphia hospital. No fungus or bacteria were found in repeated spinal fluid examinations, but her spinal fluid contained pus cells. Although Linda continued to have a low-grade fever, headaches, a stiff neck, and vomiting, the specialists were hesitant about starting her on antibiotics. However, after two months, several antibiotics were tried and one of them, when given in large doses, freed her from the fever and other troublesome symptoms. After a month on the high dosage, a spinal tap showed that the spinal fluid was normal in every respect.

Will Linda's meningeal infection return if the heavy doses of antibiotics are stopped? Someone has said that we do not know what the future holds but we do know who holds the future. Faith in loving Omnipotence allows one to say, with Paul, "Entertain no worry, but under all circumstances let your petitions be made known before God by prayer and pleading along with thanksgiving. So shall the peace of God, that surpasses all understanding, keep guard over your hearts and your thoughts in Christ Jesus."[7]

Linda, her husband, and all of us thank the Lord, not for the sorrow, but that out of our experience in the valley of the shadow of death, He has matured us and given "us an everlasting weight of glory that exceeds all calculations. . . ." As we keep taking our eyes from the visible and the transitory, endearing to us though they are, and look beyond to that which is eternal, we discover that faith can see farther through a tear than through a telescope.

CHAPTER 20

Mud or Stars?

Two men look out through the same bars:
One sees the mud, and one the stars.[1]

THIS QUOTATION WAS WRITTEN LONG BEFORE ANY OF US
kicked at the slats in our cribs. However, the medical significance of it was not sensed by scientists until the past
decade. The two men who looked through the same prison
bars reacted in widely different fashions to the stress factors in their confinement: one was frustrated by the bars,
whereas the other, subjected to the identical environment,
was inspired by the stars. The frustrated man developed
stress in his body and thus exposed himself to many serious, even fatal, diseases.

Physicians now recognize the great importance of internal stress in causing and aggravating a host of diseases.
Because all of us are subjected to a host of stresses, it
behooves us to scrutinize the subject.

Two prisoners were subjected to the same stress factors,
but only one developed inner stress and exposed himself
to disease. Examination of his blood would have revealed
the presence of abnormal chemical compounds that were
called forth as a result of his emotions of frustration, resentment, anger, hate, anxiety and fear—the same brood
of carnal emotions referred to in previous chapters.

One needs to distinguish between *inner stress,* which one
experiences in his body, and external *stress factors.* All of
us are subjected to many, many stress factors in our daily
lives, but that does not mean we have to develop inner
stress with its resultant toxic chemicals and diseases. One
of the men subjected to the external stress factors of prison
bars was actually inspired by the stars—stars he may never
have noticed before.

There are great differences in the ways people react to
stress agents such as experiencing an automobile accident,
speaking in public, disciplining a child, deciding the brand
of refrigerator to buy, chasing the neighbor's dog out of

the flower bed, or being awakened at 2 A.M. by a philandering cat. Physicians are kept busy treating people who react poorly to these and other stressful situations. Some patients develop sieges of abdominal distress that last three or four weeks and require a great deal of medication. Others suffer the agonies of severe migraine headaches, with vomiting, which incapacitate them for a day or two. A few succumb to coronary heart attacks.

On the other hand, some people who are subjected to the identical stress factors adapt so well that they experience no ill effects at all. Since we often have little control over the stress factors that daily bombard us, it is of the utmost importance that we learn to adapt properly to them if we are to save our bodies and minds from the ravages of stress and disease.

Three things must be practiced if one is to adapt successfully to life's disease-producing stressors:

1. Diversify the stressful agents
2. Avoid long exposure to such agents by resting
3. Take the proper attitude of mind.

First, it is important to remember that man can not take long or continued exposure to any one stress factor. The carpenter who pounds nails all day should not spend his evenings spading flower beds, mowing the lawn, or working in his carpentry shop. These activities would be ideal for a clerk or a lawyer.

Failure to diversify the stressful agents will sooner or later result in *fatigue,* one of the most important symptoms of stress in the body. A number of years ago I saw a diagram in a medical journal which purported to show how one could avoid fatigue. The article explained that attention should be given to three angles of life:

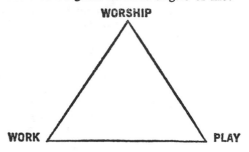

From my experience I can recall times when I worked so hard during the day that I was tempted not to go to prayer meeting because of my fatigue. Before the prayer meeting ended, however, I was surprised to find that not only had my fatigue gone, but I was rested and refreshed. Daily Bible reading, prayer and attendance at church services are of the greatest medicinal value.

Second, our attitude of mind is a most important factor in determining whether we shall suffer from exposure to life's daily stress. Our tendency in the past has been to blame our diseases on the people around us instead of blaming our troubles on our faulty reactions to those people. The sorrows and insults of daily living need not cause much trouble if we take them with the right mental attitude. Chronic brooding over sorrows and insults indicates faulty adaptation, which can cause any condition from itching feet to insanity. *The most common form of faulty reaction is self-pity.*

Actually, one shouldn't blame an unreasonable boss or teacher or marital partner for one's ulcers. Ulcers and high blood pressure are caused by internal resentments which produce toxic reactions within one's body. Take as an example my telephone, which rings dozens of times while I am trying to do a job. After the first dozen calls, I have a tendency to cringe from these repeated interruptions. Yet I know that if I allow myself to react with antagonism, the repeated ringing of a simple thing like a telephone might cause my ulcer to flare up. The stresses that hit me are not as culpable as my reaction to them. *Most of us have been guilty of generating ten dollars' worth of adrenaline over a ten-cent incident.*

In fact, while I was typing the last sentence, my telephone rang. I heard the voice of one of the college infirmary nurses: "Dr. McMillen, I have sent over to your office a girl with a dog. The dog has a fishhook in its ear. I don't know how to take it out, so I am sending her to you."

I can remember a time when my remarks to that nurse might have burned out a wire in the telephone circuit. I also know that if I had reacted with antagonism, I would have experienced a severe, pounding headache, not because of the telephone message but because of my big *reaction* to the insignificant stress—a simple, humanitarian request. A faulty reaction on my part, instead of giving me a pounding headache, could have given me a stroke of apoplexy or a fatal heart attack. Years ago my faulty adaptation to stress nearly caused my death from a bleeding ulcer.

We should remember that stress per se is usually innocent of disease causation. Furthermore, it has been shown that stress can even help to cure certain mild diseases. Dr. Hans Selye injected irritating croton oil under the skins of a large number of rats. This oil formed tender, inflammatory pouches. Selye discovered that when he subjected some of the rats to mild stresses, healing of the inflammations was hastened.[2]

I can recall many times when I had to make house calls on patients when I wasn't feeling well myself. I found out that the stress of making the trip often cured me of my minor aches and pains. However, if I had made the trip in the spirit of antagonism, my faulty reaction might have put me in the hospital for a week.

Is it not a remarkable fact that our reactions to stress determine whether stress is going to cure us or make us sick? Here is an important key to longer and happier living. We hold the key and can decide whether stress is going to work *for* us or *against* us. Our attitude decides whether stress makes us "better or bitter."

The Bible anticipated these findings by centuries. Naturally we are restless when we have to live with thorny people, or in a disagreeable environment, or when we possess aches and pains in our bodies. Thorny people, taken with a wrong attitude, can give the body any disease from boils to gallstones. Thorny people, taken with the right attitude, may free the body of certain chemicals and thus cure an illness.

Paul had a "thorn in the flesh" that gave him stress: "Thrice I invoked the Lord about this, to have it removed from me, and He told me, 'My grace is sufficient for you, for My strength comes to perfection where there is weakness.' So I am happy to take pride rather in my weaknesses, so that the power of Christ may abide upon me. I delight, therefore, in weaknesses, in insults, in needy circumstances, in persecutions and dire calamities, all on account of Christ. For when I am weak, then I am strong."[3]

There is a third factor to remember if we are to adapt successfully to the assaults of daily living: avoidance of long and continued exposure to severe stress agents, without resting. There is a limit to the stress that any person can endure, and every physician sees men and women who pay dearly in body and mind for their excessive application to work without proper rest periods. Many people could be alive today if they had heeded the admonition of Jesus to His laboring disciples: "Come ye yourselves apart into a desert place, and rest a while: for there were many coming and going, and they had no leisure so much as to eat."[4]

Many of some 31,000 Allied soldiers imprisoned in Japan and Korea in the 1940's couldn't see anything except mud. Dr. Harold Wolff states that even though these prisoners were offered enough food, "the prisoner became apathetic, listless, neither ate nor drank, helped himself in no way, stared into space and finally died." Of the 31,000 imprisoned, over 8,000 died. Dr. Wolff states that many of these deaths were caused by "despair and deprivation of human support and affection." Dr. Wolff, who is editor-in-chief of *Archives and Neurology and Psychiatry,* declares that "Hope, like faith and a purpose in life, is medicinal. This is not merely a statement of belief, but a conclusion proved by meticulously controlled scientific experiment."[5]

Another prisoner could see stars. Such a one was my esteemed Japanese friend, Dr. David Tsutada. When Japan entered World War II, the Japanese government put him in prison because of his belief in the return of the Lord to reign on this earth. The government tried to starve him to death and his weight dropped to seventy pounds. He was even confined in a cold, damp hole in a prison that was utterly filthy. As he sat on the floor, he wondered if this was the way the Lord was going to take him home to heaven. If it was, he was perfectly resigned to it. He wasn't frustrated by the bars or the mud or the Lord's apparent lack of care for him. If Dr. Tsutada had not adapted himself and resigned himself, I am convinced that the stress of self-pity, added to the severe stress of starvation, would have killed him.

While he was in prison, the Lord began to reveal to him plans for a Bible School. Dr. Tsutada worked out many details for the school while he sat in the darkness and stench of the death cell. When the war was over, he was released and immediately he put his plans into operation. Today this man has one of the finest Bible training schools in Japan. All of this transpired because he didn't fret about evildoers (Psalm 37) but trusted, committed himself to, and delighted in God's word. Dr. Tsutada created his own environment.

There were others who saw stars through prison bars. Madame Guyon reacted so well to the strain of imprisonment that out of it came writings that have inspired all Christendom.

Few people were ever behind as many bars as Helen Keller—blind, deaf and dumb—yet she became immortal in the annals of fame because she utilized her adversities as steppingstones in climbing out of her dungeon to bless a world with her spirit and love.

We should not unduly fear life's difficulties or go to great lengths to avoid them. Strong contrary winds need not blow us to destruction. In fact, the intelligent mariner can adjust his sails properly so that even adverse winds shall help him reach his goal. Contrary people can help us if we make the necessary adjustments in our mental rigging. On the water they call it *tacking,* but on land they call it *tact.*

John Bunyan forgot about the prison bars, so taken up was he with things beyond this world. He blessed not only his own soul but millions of others with that notable great seller of the centuries, *Pilgrim's Progress.* In one of his other books Bunyan gave excellent advice about preparing the mind for stresses even before they hit. Although his advice was written three hundred years ago, nothing today can surpass it:

Moreover, it is our wisdom, that while we are at ease, have our comforts about us, let us look for troubles; afflictions *from* God, as well as *for* God, are part of our cross which we must take up daily. Sickness, death of friends, loss of estate, etc., we must look for them that we may not be surprised.

So it must be our care to provide for afflictions; for to prevent them altogether we cannot; but prepare for them we may, and must, as was hinted before; to treasure up God's promises, and store our souls with graces, and spiritual comforts, and firm resolutions in God's strength, to bear up and to hold on: we need be well "shod with the preparation of the gospel of peace," Eph. 6:15.

Most Christians are not mortified and crucified to the world, not acquainted with God and the promises as they ought to be, nor so resolved to follow God fully, as they ought, and therefore are so dejected and discontented when affliction comes.[6]

Here is solid truth. Since we have shown that our attitudes of mind are more important than the daily insults of life, it is important that we condition our minds before life's major catastrophies hit us. Armies recognize this basic truth and put their troops through rigorous training. If Christians would practice such Biblical admonitions as fasting and disciplining of bodily desires, perhaps we wouldn't have so many "chocolate soldiers" who melt down when they have to undergo the hot and fierce experiences of unexpected sorrow, desertion by a mate, or financial losses.

Jacob looked at mud and grabbed for the things of mud even from the moment of his birth. He came into the world with his little baby fist reaching for the heel of his brother. As soon as he was able to trade, he created a black market on pottage and traded a little of it for his brother's birthright. He even outtricked that past master in knavery—his father-in-law.

How would you expect a character like Jacob to react to stress? When he was told that his favorite son, Joseph, had been killed, there was nothing wrong in the natural sorrow he felt, but his adaptation to the stress was very faulty because Jacob kept weeping long after he should have stopped. To those who sought to comfort him, he said, "I want to go down to the grave mourning for my son."[7] He preferred the warming balm of self-pity to facing the situations of life. The man who never learns to adjust properly to stress never becomes mature.

Jacob insisted on looking at mud instead of believing that even misfortunes can be an important part of God's blueprints, as was certainly the case with him. Jacob's insistence on protracted weeping was entirely out of order because God had actually preserved Joseph. It would appear that Jacob thought God had died, too, for his faith was so deficient that all he could do was groan, ". . . all these things are against me."[8]

He evidently suffered in his own body the results of his maladjustment, for near the close of his life, he grunted, ". . . few and strenuous my life's days and years have been and not equal to the pilgrim years of my father's. . . ."[9]

Now Paul had far more assaults to withstand than

Jacob, but he saw the stars: "Five times I received from the Jews forty lashes minus one; thrice I was cudgeled; once I was stoned; three times I was shipwrecked; for a night and a day I have been adrift at sea. In my many travels I have been in dangers of rivers and of robbers, of Jews and Gentiles, of city, desert, and sea; in dangers among sham brothers; in wearying work and hardship through many a sleepless night; in hunger, thirst, and many fastings; in cold and lack of clothing."[10] In these frightful situations did Paul ever moan, "All these things are against me?" In contrast, he exclaimed, "None of these things move me." He refused to allow self-pity to fill his body with disease-producing hormones. What was the secret of Paul's successful adaptation to these many stressful agents? Where can one obtain adaptation to repeated floggings, stonings, and deprivation of food?

We have already observed that our reactions to the unavoidable stresses of life determine whether they can cure us or kill us. Therefore, it will be highly profitable for us to analyze the *method* used and taught by the Apostle.

After listing the many stress agents that assail mankind, he gives the divine secret for successful adaptation: "Can anything separate us from the love of Christ? Can trouble, pain or persecution? Can lack of clothes and food, danger to life and limb, the threat of force of arms? Indeed some of us know the truth of that ancient text: 'For Thy sake we are killed all the day long; We were accounted as sheep for the slaughter.' No, in all these things we win an overwhelming victory through Him Who has proved His love for us."[11]

Here is the Scriptural secret for victorious adaptation to life's insults. At the beginning of each day consider yourself a sheep that is going to be abused even to the extreme of being slaughtered. If you take that attitude of mind, then nothing that comes up should frustrate or disturb you.

A man awaiting death is not disturbed by many stress factors that upset people. He is not upset because his neighbor's chickens are scratching up his flower bed; his arthritis is not worsened because the taxes on his house have been raised; his blood pressure is not raised because his employer discharged him; he doesn't get a migraine headache because his wife burned his toast; and his ulcerative colitis doesn't flair up because the stock market goes down ten points. The crucified soul is not frustrated. The man who willingly, cheerfully and daily presents himself as a "living sacrifice" can excellently adapt to the severest situations and, with Paul, be "more than conquerors. . . ."[12]

One may ask, "Isn't it foolish to give up our rights?" Perhaps it is not foolish, since in giving up our rights we insure our health and happiness. In giving up the other fellow a "piece of our mind," we always lose our peace of heart. To the natural man it is unthinkable that he should give in when he is right. He refuses to sacrifice his pride, but in so doing he sacrifices his health. Not too intelligent a transaction!

It is the spirit of retaliation that calls forth glandular toxins, and man suffers from his strong sense of self-expression and self-pity. If one takes time to analyze the cause of faulty adaptation to life's difficulties, one will often discover a little four letter word—*self*. Stress and disease result because of our unwillingness to sacrifice the big "I."

CHAPTER 21

The Nation's
No. 1 Health Problem

ABOUT NINE MILLION AMERICANS SUFFER FROM EMOTIONAL and mental illness. As many hospital beds are filled by the mentally deranged as are occupied by all medical and surgical patients combined. In fact, one out of every twenty Americans will have a psychotic disturbance severe enough to confine him in a hospital for the insane. Mental disease is indeed the nation's No. 1 health problem.

What does it cost to take care of the patients in our

mental hospitals? The annual cost is about one billion dollars. Besides, outside the asylums there are a vast number who do not need confinement but who are incapable of supporting themselves. They work little or not at all and constitute a great burden on the taxpayer.

What is the cause of mental illness? In this chapter we wish to discuss briefly those disturbances in which visible changes occur in the brain. First, an insignificant percentage of these cases are caused by direct injury to the brain in an accident. Second, brain damage may also result from an infection or a toxin. The most common infection responsible for insanity is syphilis. A score of years ago, ten per cent of the inmates of our asylums were put there by syphilis.

By far the most common toxin responsible for insanity is alcohol. From the 1959 edition of *A Textbook of Medicine,* we read: "About 10% of the admissions to mental hospitals are officially reported as due to alcoholism and another 10% have alcoholism of considerable degree reported as an important contributing cause. In addition, general hospitals take care of many of the acutely disturbed alcoholics, and there is an unknown but large number of persons . . . who are ruining their careers and undergoing a sort of gradual personality suicide through addiction to alcohol."[1]

The third common type of insanity that involves visible changes in the brain is arteriosclerosis of the cerebral arteries. In a previous chapter we noted the important factors causing arteriosclerosis, such as heredity, eating of animal fat, overeating, smoking and stress. However, these frequent mental disturbances in the elderly are often due to a combination of arteriosclerosis and a personality factor. Some elderly people may suffer from a frank insanity but often, instead of being considered insane, they are better described as "impossible." The unlovely personality that develops in some senior citizens is not a sudden onset. It is rather the continuation of childhood temper tantrums, the elaboration of teenage assertiveness, the further development of middle-aged orneriness which has now fully developed into the thorny, sour and crabbed frustrations of old age.

Before arteriosclerosis started to clog his cerebral arteries, the peppery outbreaks of this individual were endurable only because they were spread over a variety of contacts and lasted for a short time. Now that arteriosclerosis has radically reduced his physical activities, changed his bluster to obstreperousness and concentrated it within the four walls of one house, he has become impossible.

If we lead cranky, complaining and censorious lives down through the years, then pity our children when the ugliness of our bad personalities is multiplied and aggravated by the clogging of our cerebral arteries. It may be as difficult to change our attitudes as it is to change a deep groove in a phonograph record, and if we are not careful now, we may end up as a two-legged bore.

Dr. Bess Fancher, a keen observer of people, once said to me, "Doctor, we don't have much to say about how we look at sixteen. But we are the ones who determine how we are going to look at sixty." William Wordsworth expressed the same thought in another way: "The child is father of the man."[2]

Typical of the attitude of those who have the care of their elderly parents are the words of Mrs. Sabin: "Doctor, you must tell me what I am going to do with Mom. I simply can't take any more. She had us up most of the night. My husband got about one half hour's sleep and then had to go to work. I find myself yelling at the children and they are upset. After these years of having my mother here, I am completely worn out. Even the sleeping capsules don't help her any more. Doctor, I am bushed. I have had it! You must do something!"

Needless to say, physicians have no easy solution for some of these problems. Hospitals and nursing homes don't want troublesome patients because they disturb others, and relatives are always loathe to put their loved ones in a mental institution. Actually, these cases aren't serious enough for an asylum, but they are too difficult for any other place. If they live long enough many of them do end up there. Some of these people fray the patience and shorten the lives of those who are ministering to them.

Lest I give the wrong impression of old age, I hasten to describe a man in his nineties, one of the grandest men I ever knew. Throughout the many years I knew him, he always displayed kindness, cheerfulness and consideration for everybody. When Reverend D. B. Hampe retired from an active, successful ministry in Akron, Ohio, he was, in his words, "ninety-two years young." For many years he refused to be superannuated because he said he was "superanimated." He was, and he had more vision and energy than some men thirty years younger.

After his retirement, Reverend Hampe and his crippled wife went to live with their married daughter. Some time later, he had a number of "little strokes," the comas lasting a few minutes to a few hours. Then a severe stroke hit him. The coma lasted for several days and deepened. He was not able to swallow. To prolong his days which, even in his illness, seemed to radiate a blessing to those around him, I passed a stomach tube and thus supplied him with nourishment. Once more he became partly conscious. He sensed what we were doing to keep him alive, smiled a bit, and said, "I think it would be better if you would let me go home to be with the Lord."

A day or two later we tried to talk to him in his semi-comatose state. He seemed to hear, although he couldn't open his eyes or talk, but he did summon up the last particles of his strength to raise a feeble hand to wave good-by.

Six years have now passed and his wife is still living in their daughter's home. Mrs. Hampe will soon be ninety-four. Though badly crippled and confined largely to a chair, she is always happy and cheerful. When food is brought on her tray, she says, "That looks good," or makes some other complimentary remark. She has plenty of aches and pains but never mentions them.

What is the reason for the contrast between this couple and others even much younger? To my mind the answer is evident. They obeyed Biblical injunctions and saved themselves from many of the factors that cause arteriosclerosis. Not only did they live a long time, but they developed choice personalities because they took the Bible as their guide. For fifty-five years they served the Lord in their unselfish devotion to help others. Often, on small ministerial appointments, they eked out an existence for themselves and their four children. No arteriosclerotic plaques developed in them from overeating, and they always took what the Lord gave them with happy, thankful hearts.

Little wonder that this crippled widow is loved by all who know her. Her daughter and the in-laws with whom she lives never feel burdened with her but thank the Lord for keeping her alive to refresh their own souls.

The Bible has hundreds of helpful suggestions for long, happy and sane living. Here is one of them:

Come, listen to me, my sons,
    I will teach you true religion.
Tis your desire to live,
    to live long and be happy?
Then keep your tongue from evil,
    keep your lips from deceit;
    shun evil and do good,
    seek to be friendly—aim at that.[8]

In those few lines there is medical therapy that would prevent millions of cases of mental illness. ". . . shun evil . . ."—the perfect prophylaxis against syphilitic paresis, formerly the cause of one out of every ten cases in our asylums. ". . . shun evil . . ."—and avoid alcoholic psychosis, which currently tops the list in admissions to our mental institutions.

"Then keep your tongue from evil, keep your lips from deceit, . . . do good, seek to be friendly . . ."—there you have advice that, if followed, would save one from becoming a censorious whiner. Doing friendly acts to others always develops a personality that is lovely and fragrant. If tens of thousands in our institutions today had developed such Scriptural attitudes, they would not be kicking out their last tantrums in asylums and nursing homes.

CHAPTER 22

Snails and Schizophrenics

ROSEMARY WAS DEMURE, RESERVED, AND GAVE METICULOUS attention to herself and her clothes. She patterned herself after her mother, who was "fluffily feminine." On a summer day one could find Rosemary sitting in the garden, weaving garlands of flowers. She did not go out of her way to mix with others. As a young child she read a great deal, and the knights and ladies of King Arthur's court seemed more real to her than anyone else. As she grew older her ideals were always fictional characters, devoid of faults and much more glamorous than ordinary people who sometimes said nasty things.

When Rosemary went away to college she became unhappy. At home she had had a room of her own, but in the dormitory she shared a room with two other girls—girls far removed from Jane Austen's heroines. Her roommates and classmates sensed Rosemary's unconscious shrinking from them and labeled her "stuckup." She slept poorly, was constipated, did not exercise, and could not take any interest in her environment.

One morning Rosemary did not get up. A little past noon she was still in bed while her breakfast and luncheon trays remained untouched. To the questions of the dormitory dean she gave only a vacant stare. She was as motionless and stiff as a wax figure.

She was taken to the college infirmary, where she required more care than a baby. Food that was placed in her mouth remained there, and liquid nourishment had to be given through a small stomach tube. Previously very immaculate about her hygiene, she now had to be washed and the bedding had to be changed frequently. When her mother arrived, Rosemary did not recognize her.

The most surprising characteristic of Rosemary's affliction was that an attendant could place her body or limbs in any awkward position and they remained fixed. Within a few hours an intelligent girl with good scholastic grades had changed to a motionless, waxy figure incapable of helping herself in any way. Dr. Melvin Thorner presents this case as a typical illustration of schizophrenia.[1]

Schizophrenia is the most common form of insanity, accounting for twenty-three per cent of first admissions to state hospitals. These patients require longer hospitalizations than those with any other mental condition; hence fifty per cent of the half million patients in our mental hospitals are schizophrenic cases. The age of onset is usually between eighteen and thirty-five years of age.

Not all patients come down with this malady as did Rosemary. Psychiatrists divide schizophrenics into four or more different types. Since it is one of the most difficult mental conditions to cure after it is fully developed, and since there is much we can do to prevent it, we should take a closer look at this dreary affliction.

Actually, before Rosemary became frankly insane, her mind was split between a pleasant fictional world of glamorous people and an unpleasant world of reality. Because of these *two* worlds in which she lived, we refer to her condition as *schizophrenia (schizo,* "to split," and *phrenia,* "the mind").

A look at the snail will help one to understand this lamentable form of insanity. A snail has such a timid personality that he never comes completely out of his shell. Even when he has to emerge a little, he is fearful and unhappy. Slowly he raises two little periscopes equipped with eyes on top and looks around very shyly. If things seem favorable, he projects a bit of himself into the fearsome world of reality and then laboriously pulls his stony, spiraled castle after him. If the world becomes threatening in any degree, he retracts every bit of himself into his shell. There he may stay inordinately long, even after the danger has disappeared.

Of course, all of us who glory in our normality must confess that we sometimes retreat into our shells, a reaction which is properly protective. However, we need to be careful lest our retreat inward, to suckle comfort from self-pity, become too frequent an occurrence. Unless we exercise caution, we shall spend too much time daydreaming and lolling in the lovely labyrinths of fantasy. Certainly, if we continue to brood and lick the sores of our wounded pride rather than push ourselves outward to face the realities of a cold, factual world, or if we form the habit of withdrawal every time the going gets hard, our personalities may become as twisted as the spirals of a snail's shell.

Depending on the degree of our withdrawal, people will refer to us as the dreamy type, or an introvert, or a shut-in personality, or a queer soul, or finally a schizophrenic.

Schizophrenia is a specific reaction to severe anxiety arising from inability to meet the demands of adult adjustment.[2] Anxiety in the emotional center can result in various glands being stimulated with the formation of abnormal chemicals. These chemicals, acting on the brain, may be responsible for abnormal mental disturbances. Supporting this view are the changes that occur in a dog when a chemical, bulbocapnine, is injected. These changes are surprisingly similar to those that occurred in Rosemary. An injected dog refuses to eat or drink, does not recognize old friends, and has the same waxy rigidity of the legs. Furthermore, chemists have proved that the injection of other chemicals can cause psychotic hallucinations or feeblemindedness. Dr. Carl Jung was the first to teach that the cause of schizophrenia was a toxin injurious to the brain—said toxin being formed by emotional disturbance, especially anxiety.

In some cases, heredity appears to make some people more likely to develop schizophrenia. However, an individual who has a number of schizophrenics in his background certainly should not be unduly upset. Anyone who has inherited a lot of dynamite in his cerebral attic should remember that this dynamite is dangerous only when it is exposed to the hot sparks of emotional fire. Such a person should know that heredity does not *cause* schizophrenia, but may be a *predisposing* factor. Hence, it would be wise for one who has a schizophrenic heredity to exercise more than average caution to avoid anxiety and stressful situations.

Also very important as a predisposing factor is environment. An individual whose home, community or occupation is loaded with stressful situations should exercise more care. Supporting this view is a study of 263 schizophrenics who improved and were released from asylums. Analysis of the patients who had a recurrence of their insanity revealed that the most common cause of relapse was emotional conflict in the environment.

Parents are big factors in helping their children to adjust smoothly to the outside world, and it is obvious that they too play a role in the development of schizophrenia. The parents of Rosemary had done little to prepare her for entrance to college. Her life was centered in daisy chains and novels. Because other children did not allow her to have her own way, she avoided them, and her parents, instead of training her to give in, had taken her part in her conflicts. Perhaps Rosemary's parents had read that frustrations were bad and had catered to her every whim. She had never been made to work, so her physical activity was almost nil.

We do not understand the chemistry involved, but it is a well-recognized fact that physical work is both a preventive and curative factor in a number of mental disturbances. Many a mother washes the dishes with the excuse, "I would rather do them myself than go through all the fuss of making Milly do them." Such a remark indicates maternal failure and may forecast a personality disturbance for Milly.

Suppose Darlene has been jilted by her high-school boy-friend. The best thing to free her from the deleterious effects of toxic brooding is physical activity. There is no better psychotherapeutic appliance than the common scrub brush.

Pity the youngster who is not required to work. An indulgent father shovels the snow off the walks and driveway because Junior didn't get in until late last night. As a result Dad threatens himself with a coronary attack while six-foot Junior spends the entire morning sleeping. Junior is given all the time he wants to build castles in the air, but he has never been taught to build a woodshed on the ground.

Psychiatry recognizes that laziness is a frequent characteristic of schizophrenics. Dr. William S. Sadler writes, "Many of these cases are youths who are not disposed to accept the social restrictions and the cultural demands of their environments."[3] They are unwilling to put forth constructive efforts to adapt because it is so much easier to get away from work and real people by withdrawing themselves into the twisted spirals of their fantasies.

A boy who is given a program of work is not likely to turn into a hoodlum who goes around chopping up pianos and furniture for "thrills." Neither is he likely to dent the family income to pay for treatment by a psychiatrist. A more effective treatment, if he is not too old, would be a visit to the family woodshed and the warm application of this Biblical wisdom: "Foolishness is bound up in the heart of a child; But the rod of correction shall drive it far from him."[4]

People are still talking about a Houghton College commencement address delivered many years ago by Dr. James S. Luckey on the subject of the neglected command, "Six days shalt thou labor. . . ."[5] I suspect John Smith lessened the possibilities for schizophrenia in the early Jamestown colony because he enforced another Scriptural directive: ". . . this we commanded you, that if any would not work, neither should he eat."[6]

Parental fear of frustrating a youngster often produces an undisciplined teen-ager who is an easy prey for life's frustrations. About ten years ago I was called to a college infirmary to see an eighteen-year-old girl whom I shall call Lorna Henderson. She was partly withdrawn, responded poorly to questioning, and kept fearfully exclaiming, "I am two people, and I don't know which one to listen to!"

From her classmates I discovered that she had lost a great deal of sleep because of studying for midterm examinations and also because she had wanted to participate in a number of social engagements. She was the holder of an excellent scholarship, which meant that her marks had to stay in the upper brackets.

Lorna and her roommate had been arguing. Then, three days before her mental breakdown, she and her fiancè had quarreled. Cumulative anxiety did something inside her and she withdrew from cruel reality.

The next day her parents arrived and came to my office for a conference. With them were two other children about seven and nine years of age. During our interview these two children moved everything that was movable in my office. The refined and educated parents made many verbal remonstrances but nothing more. In return the little boy kicked his mother in the shins and several times the girl spit at her father.

I am reminded of what Dr. Douglas Kelly, University of California professor and chief psychiatrist at the Nuremberg trials, said: "Spare the Freud and save the child." He said the fear of repressing the child has run wild through modern education and child rearing. The result, in his words, is: "A generation of children who have not been taught the discipline required for getting along with the world. . . . We have been overenthusiastic in our refusal to teach control lest we traumatize."[7]

If Lorna did not meet frustration when she was five, ten and fifteen years old at home, it is quite understandable why she was incapable of coping in a strange environment with the frustrations caused by a roommate, by her inability to get high grades, and by her fiancè's desertion. *Children who have never been conditioned by some frustrations during the first fifteen years of life will not be very fit to meet the demands of adult living without experiencing unusual stress, with its abnormal and potent chemicals.*

Finally, the individual himself is a tremendous factor in determining whether schizophrenia develops. True, he has nothing to say about his heredity, often not much more to say about his environment and the type of parental training he receives. If all these have been exceptionally bad, he may have a difficult task trying to change the mold in which he was cast. Yet to a considerable extent he is the captain and can direct his course. Forty years ago I knew a young woman whose heredity, environment and parental training were deplorable. Today she possesses a beautifully integrated personality. Everyone who knows her will affirm that her excellent qualities and transformation have been due to following Christ.

The individual who has Christ in his heart and the Bible in his hand has splendid fortifications against man's greatest mental disturbance—schizophrenia. Why do I make that statement? It is medically recognized that schizophrenia is the result of anxiety stemming from an inability to meet the adjustments of adulthood. In highly predisposed individuals even a little anxiety can tip the scales. Furthermore, it is felt that any individual, if subjected to sufficient stress, could experience the schizophrenic reaction.

Naturally, anything that lessens anxiety is important in the prevention of schizophrenia. In reduction of anxiety, nothing is more important than spiritual conversion and Christian living. Anyone who ever truly repented his sins and asked God to forgive him can never forget the miraculous way in which his mind was immediately freed of "the guilt complex." Whether the offense is trivial or enormous, Christ immediately forgives and brings a peace "which passeth all understanding. . . ."[8] Millions can testify to the veracity of His promise: "Peace I leave with you; my peace I give unto you: not as the world giveth, give I unto you. Let not your heart be troubled, neither let it be fearful."[9]

Since the schizophrenic patient is suffering because his interest and energies are directed inward, it is not surprising to read: "The objective is to . . . detach his emotions from subjective material, redirect his interests to things outside himself, inculcate healthful social habits. . . ."[10] The Bible gave this same advice centuries before: "None of you should think only of his own affairs, but should learn to see things from other people's point of view."[11]

Certainly Lorna had neither been taught nor had she picked up the self-discipline that is necessary for getting along with people in this world. Because she couldn't get along with her fiancè, he had broken their engagement. Consecrated Christians spell disappointments with a capital H—*His appointments*. Actually Lorna was partly to blame, for she had created much of the emotional hurricane that swamped her. She had been unwilling to accept any frustrations from anyone, so intent was she on having her own self-centered way. One cannot help wondering if things would not have been different had she been living out these Scriptural admonitions:

Let there be no more resentment, no more anger or temper, no more violent self-assertiveness, no more slander and no more malicious remarks. Be kind to each other, be understanding. Be as ready to forgive others as God for Christ's sake has forgiven you.[12]

Let us have real warm affection . . . and a willingness to let the other man have the credit.[13]

So let us concentrate on the things which make for harmony, and on the growth of one another's character.[14]

I have seen Christians in their zeal for the Lord become guilty of another fault that Lorna had—they attempt too much. One must have time for rest and relaxation: "And he [Jesus] saith unto them, Come ye yourselves apart into a desert place, and rest a while. For there were many coming and going, and they had not leisure so much as to eat."[15]

Lorna, in her anxiety to keep up her grades, studied seven days a week. She didn't think the Biblical command to rest one day in seven was for her and her generation. She didn't sense that the worth of this regulation has been amply confirmed by modern research workers studying stress. Lorna, like thousands of others, never learned that a loving Father gave these admonitions for the sake of saving His children from physical and mental disturbances.

From the moment man sinned and brought upon himself bodily and mental diseases, the Lord sought to succor him and mitigate the effects of diseases. But man, with his perverted mind, has often brushed aside as worthless the very admonitions that could have saved him. In view of the factors mentioned in the prevention of schizophrenia, we can clearly see a Father's love shining through the commands to work, to rest, to "learn to see things from other people's point of view," to see to it that "there be no more resentment, no more anger or temper, no more violent self-assertiveness," and to open the door of our hearts so that the Holy Comforter may enter. Since we have learned that schizophrenia is "a specific reaction to severe anxiety," we can understand the emphasis Jesus and the Apostles placed on the infilling of man with the Holy Spirit who is the personification of peace. "Peace I leave with you; my peace I give unto you. . . ."

CHAPTER 23

A Lesson From John D.

AS A YOUNG MAN, JOHN D. ROCKEFELLER, SR., WAS AS strong and husky as a farm lad. When he entered business he drove himself harder than any slave was ever driven by the whip of a taskmaster. At the early age of thirty-three, he had made his first million dollars. By consecrating every waking moment to his work, he controlled, at forty-three, the biggest business in the world. When he was fifty-three, he was the richest man on earth and the world's only billionaire.

For this achievement he had bartered his own happiness and health. He developed alopecia, a condition in which not only the hair of the head drops off but also most of the hair from the eyelashes and eyebrows. One of his biographers said that he looked like a "mummy." His weekly income was a million dollars, but his digestion was so bad that he could eat only crackers and milk.

Like Scrooge, John D. was as solitary as an oyster. He once confessed that he "wanted to be loved," but did not sense that people love only those who emanate affection. Lacking in consideration for others, he had often crushed the helpless into the mire in his lust to make bigger profits. So hated was he in the oil fields of Pennsylvania that the men whom he had pauperized hanged him in effigy, and he had bodyguards day and night. The mass of wealth he had accumulated gave him neither peace nor happiness. In fact, as he sought to protect and control it, he discovered that he was being smothered by it. He could not sleep; he enjoyed nothing.

When John D. was only fifty-three, Ida Tarbell wrote of him, "An awful age was in his face. He was the oldest man that I have ever seen." The crackers and milk he glumly swallowed could no longer hold together his skinny body and restless soul. It was generally agreed that he would not live another year, and newspaper writers had his obituary written and ready in their files.

Then John D. began to do some thinking in the long nights when he couldn't sleep. One night he made a startling discovery: *he would not be able to take even one of his thin dimes with him into the next world!* His was the despair and helplessness of the little boy who sees the relentless tide coming in to sweep into oblivion all the sand castles he has been building.

For the first time in his life he recognized that money was not a commodity to be hoarded but something to be shared for the benefit of others. In the morning he, like Scrooge, lost no time in transforming his money into blessings to others. He began to help worthy causes. He established the Rockefeller Foundation so that some of his fortune could be channeled to needed areas. It would require a book to describe the benefits that resulted from the many hundreds of millions of dollars that he showered on universities, hospitals, mission work, and millions of underprivileged people. He was the one who helped rid the South of its greatest economic and physical scourge— hookworm. We can thank John D. every time our lives and the lives of our children are saved by an injection of penicillin because his contributions aided in the discovery of this miracle drug. His money sparked the research that saved and is still saving millions of people from untimely deaths from malaria, tuberculosis, diphtheria and many other diseases.

It is not my purpose to detail the blessings the world received when John D. changed the current of his thinking from *getting* to *giving*. My object is to tell you that when he began to think *outwardly* toward the needs of others, a miracle occurred. He began to sleep, to eat normally, and to enjoy life in general. The bitterness, rancor and the deadness of self-centeredness went out of his life, and into the soul of John D. came refreshing streams of love and gratitude from those whom he was helping. He who had been repulsive and lifeless now teemed with vibrancy and activity.

When Rockefeller was fifty-three, it certainly appeared that he would never celebrate another birthday, but he started to practice one of God's eternal laws, and he reaped its promised benefits: ". . . give, and it shall be given unto you; good measure, pressed down, shaken together, running over, shall they give into your bosom."[1] He proved the value of this promise for he lived not only until his fifty-fourth and fifty-fifth birthdays, but he experienced "the good measure . . . running over"—he lived until he was ninety-eight years old.

Modern psychiatry is also catching up with the numerous and valuable Biblical admonitions to think outwardly in helpfulness toward others. One psychiatrist writes, "Without love, we lose the will to live. Our mental and physical vitality is impaired, our resistance is lowered, and we succumb to illnesses that often prove fatal. We may escape death, but what remains is a meager and barren existence, emotionally so impoverished that we can only be called half alive."[2]

Those well-known observers of human nature, Harry and Bonaro Overstreet, have written, ". . . it is one of the basic facts of human life that the ungiven self is the unfulfilled self."[3]

As human beings we take very good care of our bodies with medicine, physical examinations, vitamins, and with dozens of other aids, but we are sadly ignorant of certain mental exercises that are necessary for full-orbed happy living. Ideally, this training to think outwardly should begin at birth. Unfortunately, a tiny baby is trained to think inwardly and to sense his own importance when his parents and grandparents rush to cuddle him every time he makes the slightest fuss. They rush to the crib, pick him up, give him a bottle or a pacifier, walk the floor, or do something to let him know that sun, moon and stars are ready to answer his every beck and squall. A baby becomes so accustomed to having everything rise

and set according to his cry that, with the passing of
months and years, he cleverly perfects his technique for
keeping the current of interests directly inwardly, *ad
nauseam.*

As a first-grader in school, he reports to his parents
that a smaller boy called him a "sissy." So when he knocks
the boy down and kicks him in the face, the doting father
chuckles and applauds, "Good boy!" When the sixth-
grader wails, "That old principal punished me just for
nothing at all!" doesn't the average parent judge the case
on the plea of the juvenile plaintiff? My father never had
to judge any of my pleas because I knew that if he
heard I was punished at school I would automatically get
a whipping at home. My father might be called unreasonable, yet his method did much to prevent my self-
centeredness.

Parents who everlastingly throw mud at their neighbors'
doorsteps in order to make their own look cleaner are
setting a vicious example which their children usually
follow. Parents should not blame their children for developing sour personalities if the dining table becomes
an autopsy slab on which the neighbors are dissected.

Far too much of our efforts and money are directed
inwardly, to build up the egos of our children. We buy
eight-year-old Susie more expensive clothes than the
family budget can afford, make her "fluffily feminine," á
la Rosemary, foster the spirit of selfishness in her, buy
a piano and other instruments, give her music lessons,
but never make any worthwhile effort to get her to think
outwardly toward others.

Positive outward thinking is possible. We can buy Susie
a cake mix and have her bake and frost a cake to take to
an overworked or sick mother. What better investment
can one make with so little money to give Susie happiness
and a flying start down the road to joyful living and mental
health? Some of the loveliest personalities I know are
little children who sacrifice candy-money so that they
may give to missions and the underprivileged. Children
trained early to be considerate of others are not very
likely to cause heartbreak to parents and others in the
years ahead.

The parent is really wise who can guide fourteen-year-
old Junior to go over to a needy neighbor to mow the
lawn, rake the leaves, or shovel snow. There is no better

way to inculcate healthful social habits. From where I sit it seems that parents are going the opposite way when they equip three-year-old Keith with gun belt and six shooters to bang-bang at every passing person, and thus accustom him to the idea of getting what he wants by hurting, even killing, other people.

Because we have allowed the six-month-old baby to be *all lungs,* the ten-year-old to be *all play,* the teen-aged boy to be *all competitive sports,* the teen-aged girl to be *all fluffs and frills,* the thirty-five-year-olds *all business or bridge,* the forty-five-year-olds *all middle,* is it any wonder that the fifty-five-year-olds are *all frustrations,* and the sixty-year-olds are *all in?*

John D. Rockefeller proved that healthful, enjoyable living is not obtained by *grabbing* but by *giving* to others. When grateful citizens of Cleveland, Ohio, congratulated him, he spoke from his own experience: "Turn your thoughts upon the higher things of life. Be of service to humanity. Turn your thoughts into channels of usefulness; look forward to a determination that something useful shall come out of your success. Let your question be, 'What shall be the fruitage of my career? Shall it be the endowment of hospitals, churches, schools and asylums?' . . . . *Do everything you can for the betterment of your fellow-men and in doing this you will enjoy life the better.*"[4]

For Rockefeller, it took over a half century of sickly, wretched living and learning the hard way before he found one of the basic secrets to real life. It is pathetic indeed that earlier he did not read and heed the healthful admonitions given in the Book of books:

One who is not loving remains in death.[5]

Harmonize with others in your thinking. . . .[6]

Don't become snobbish but take a real interest in ordinary people. Don't become set in your own opinions.[7]

It is not easy for anybody to practice these directives in his own strength. Modern psychiatry may be close to the Bible in appreciating the importance of directing the current of thinking outwardly, yet psychiatry ordinarily can not provide sufficient motivating force to get any flow past unlovely obstructions—such as the powerful odor in my waiting room one night. It emanated from diapers that had not been properly washed before being put back on a two-month-old baby. The baby's mother, about thirty years old, had had nine pregnancies and seven of her children were living. She was dirty, slouchy and poor. In her hand she held several rags that she used as diapers.

I am ashamed to acknowledge the fact, but if I had not had the grace of God in my heart, I would have asked her, after taking care of the baby, to look elsewhere for future medical attention. The mental strain of trying to keep alive such a family under such filthy and difficult circumstances was more than I wanted. Why then should I become entangled again with them?

But I did. How could I do otherwise when I remembered how Jesus left the glories of heaven and came to earth because I sorely needed physical, mental and spiritual help? He came, even though the odor of my sins must have been utterly revolting to His nostrils. The cost that He paid to help me could never be measured.

Yes, psychiatry shows me the great importance of thinking outwardly toward other people, but only Christ provides sufficient motivation. He also provides the power: "For whosoever will save his life shall lose it: And whosoever will lose his life for my sake shall find it."[8]

". . . for my sake . . ."—there is the power, and there is the motivation that can save us from deadly self-centeredness.

CHAPTER 24

Don't Shoot for the Moon

"DADDY, I WANT TO GO TO THE MOON." THOSE WERE THE words of my three-year-old daughter Linda as we sat on our open terrace in Africa. One could hardly blame her, because the big tropical moon looked very, very close and resembled an enthralling fairy land. I carefully and patiently explained to her that the moon was much farther away than it appeared. In fact, no one had yet been able to go there.

Linda's desire to go was so intense that it closed her mind to every word of explanation. She continued to plead excitedly and completely ignored my helplessness. Exasperated with me, she broke into tears and wept, "Daddy, you don't even try! Go bring the dining table out here. Pile another table on it, and then all the chairs in the house, on the top of each other."

Finally she worked herself and me into a lather of mental frenzy. My last words were neither famous nor psychologically outstanding, but they were effective: "Linda, if you don't stop pestering me to take you to the moon, I'll give you a good smacking!"

When I recall her taut emotions, I can easily understand why strivings for places of eminence, with their consequent frustrations, are potent precipitating factors in the causation of mental disturbances. There are far more than mythical and etymological connections between *lunar* strivings and *lunacy*.

We shall call her Arlene Traubel. She is not one girl but a composite of about five girls I have known as patients. Arlene was a college senior and had been on the Dean's List from the time she was a freshman, a feat somewhat comparable to going to the moon. She gloated over seeing her name in that coveted column, but in her

senior year she began to feel herself slipping. The thought
of being dropped from that list after all those years made
her anxious, panicky, and decreased her ability to concentrate on her studies.

Then one day Arlene entered the infirmary because she
couldn't read. She could pronounce words but was completely unable to understand what they meant. A week
passed, with little improvement. Each day increased her
anxiety because it lessened her chances of corraling those
elusive A's.

She was sure there was something physically wrong
with her. Even though I told her that she needed more
relaxation and play as well as a changed viewpoint about
striving for the moon, she returned to her home, where
she was thoroughly examined in a hospital. She emerged
with a large bill and a diagnosis of "somatic conversion
symptoms," which means in five-cent words that her
inability to read was caused by mental turmoil. Anxiety
about her grades had manifested itself by a withdrawal
symptom—and inability to read.

Psychic turmoil, arising out of our desires to go to the
moon or to attain superiority over our fellows, is very
common. An outstanding psychiatrist, Dr. Alfred Adler,
taught that most modern nervous and emotional disorders
grow out of a definite striving for power.[1] Because the
average man in his mad drive for power is in a daily
race with others for earthly goals, his day is full of
failures, frustrations, banged-up feelings and, often, fenders.

The next time you feel unduly fatigued because life's
race has been unusually rough and bumpy, stop and
analyze the events and conversation of the foregoing hours.
Ninety-nine times out of a hundred you will discover that
someone recently let the air out of your ego. We suffer
rough going, mental weariness, exhaustion and disease,
not because of the work we do, but because we con-
sciously or subconsciously try to prove to ourselves and
to our fellows that our ideals are superior, our doctrines
are the correct ones, our church is the best, our city is
the choicest, our state is the most important, our political
concepts and party are necessary to save the world from
destruction, our ball team is going to win the world
series, and our, our, our—you name it, and we will argue
until we are blue in the face that *we* are the people and
that at our demise wisdom will surely vanish from the

earth. It is a wonder that we don't more often blow a cerebral fuse.

Last week a young man came to my office with a large hemorrhage in his eye. Nobody had punched him. The blood vessel in his eye had broken because he had developed too much blood pressure while playing the high soprano parts on his horn. Remember that young man the next time you are tempted "to toot your horn."

Is it not a pity that we are cursed with an innate urge to be ever madly racing with one another like the participants in a stock car race? In our excitement to be first we become oblivious to the damage we inflict on others and ourselves. The stock cars that are battered, banged, dented, and noisy are no worse off than bruised humanity broken down with many a disease from life's competitions.

Here are only a few of many New Testament admonitions—or, more accurately, prescriptions—that would save millions of crushed and broken hearts if people had enough faith to swallow and assimilate them:

Don't cherish exaggerated ideas of yourself or your importance, but try to have a sane estimate of your capabilities. . . .[2]

Let your love be perfectly sincere . . . allowing one another to enjoy preference of honor . . . do not aspire to eminence, but willingly adjust yourselves to humble situations; do not become wise in your own conceits.[3]

Don't aim at adding to the number of teachers, . . . I beg you! Remember that we who are teachers will be judged by a much higher standard.[4]

Live together in harmony, live together in love, as though you had only one mind and one spirit between you. Never act from motives of rivalry or personal vanity, but in humility think more of each other than you do of yourselves.[5]

Before the disciples had crucified their urge for power, which Dr. Adler calls the "ego ambition," their main drive had been to sit in places of authority and prominence and to be the greatest in the Kingdom. Speaking of the Pharisees and scribes, Jesus said:

They increase the size of their phylacteries and lengthen the tassels of their robes; they love seats of honour at dinners and front places in the synagogues. They love to be greeted with respect in public places and to have men call them "Rabbi!" Don't you ever be called "Rabbi"—

you have only one Teacher, and all of you are brothers. . . . And you must not let people call you "leaders"—you have only one leader, Christ! The only "superior" among you is the one who serves the others. For every man who promotes himself will be humbled, and every man who learns to be humble will find promotion.[6]

This Scriptural teaching is diametrically opposed to the philosophies of the world. Jesus very forcibly warns us against aspiring to leadership. His teaching does not give us any excuse whatsoever for laziness but rather exhorts that proper motivation and direction be given to the expenditure of our energies. The teaching of Jesus translated into college language is: Don't get your heart set on being a four-pointer or being on the Dean's List. Don't lose sleep over being selected queen, don't try to be the leader of any class, any committee, or anything else. Graduate work is necessary but don't "lengthen the tassels" on your robes. Don't, for the sake of the degrees, "lengthen the tassel" on the end of your name. In God's Book, "The only 'superior' among you is the one who serves the others."

Going back to medical considerations, you may wonder why the individual working to be a four-pointer suffers in his body and mind while another student, working just as hard, is free from such injuries. The student who is striving for the coveted A's and for the pre-eminence they will give him is actually digging a channel to direct the current of interests toward himself. His egocentric life, with no outflow, will be bitter and senseless. He will suffer from self-intoxication. He who refuses the Biblical injunction to adjust himself to "humble situations" will soon discover that his associates will take it upon themselves to make the necessary adjustments to him in a fashion that may be crude and heartless. The stress he then suffers can cause plenty of trouble in mind or body.

In contrast, the individual who practices God's Word is spared many bodily insults. The psalmist wrote, "Great peace have they which love thy law: and nothing shall offend them."[7] Nothing? I can't imagine greater stress than being thrown into a fire. Yet I know people, and you know people, who were thrown in and they emerged without having the smoke of fire on their garments.

Everybody meets frustration every day, but the Christian need never become frustrated. A number of times I have seen Stephen W. Paine face frustrating and personally embarrassing situations as a college president. Each time my soul has been refreshed when he said, "It is perfectly all right. Perhaps the Lord sent it to keep me humble." The man who thus yields quickly to being knocked down is not as likely to be knocked out.

There is another big difference between the individual who is seeking great things for himself and the one whose energies are devoted to God's Kingdom. In our world of business the individual who is self-employed has only his own resources to fall back upon when he meets trouble. But the man who is a vital part of a large corporation has all the resources of a billion-dollar company. Hence, he has a sense of security in knowing that, regardless of what happens, he doesn't have to worry. Doesn't it go without saying that the man or woman who is faithfully devoting his energies to a corporation that owns the cattle on a thousand hills, the oil in a million wells, and the silver, gold, and jewels in a billion solar systems, has a sense of security and freedom from frustration and disease that nothing else in this old world can ever give?

Not only is he free from worries, insults, antagonisms, and disease-producing insults incident to self-seeking, but he is granted a pleasing personality denied to those who shoot for the moon. Some time ago I read about a young woman who wanted to go to college. Her heart sank when she read one question on the application blank: "Are you a leader?" Being a conscientious girl she wrote "No" and sent in the form with a heavy heart. To her surprise she received a letter from one of the college officials which read something like this: "A study of the application blanks reveals that this year our college will have 1452 leaders. Therefore, we are accepting you because we feel it is imperative that they have *one* follower."

We are living in a day when it is not difficult to find people who want to be head cook, but few are available to wash dishes. There are always several hundreds of girls who yearn to ride in the parade as the beautiful queen, but sometimes only a disgruntled half dozen will agree to decorate the float. Organizations have never lacked those who want to be boss carpenters, but they have had to search for men to drive nails and saw boards.

Medical statistics show that it will be the whistling ditchdigger who will be digging the grave for the distraught business manager. Maybe, in our striving for the moon, we aren't too smart, after all. I grant you, it must be a thrill to shoot for the moon in an upholstered space capsule. Yet, that capsule bears an uncanny similarity to an asylum's padded cell.

Jesus said something that few people took seriously because it was as high above our earthly thinking as the heavens are above the earth. He said, ". . . the meek . . . shall inherit the earth."[8] We can believe that the meek will inherit heaven when they die, but Jesus was trying to tell us that the meek are going to inherit the earth here and now. Study the meek people you know, and you will discover that they are actually coming into possession of everything that is worth while on this earth.

With a little reflection you can understand why the meek inherit the earth. They have been thoughtful and considerate of your interests, they have been slow to talk about their great accomplishments and quick to congratulate you on your minor achievements. Down through the years they have always laughed at your "corny" jokes. Yes, you will gladly give them what you possess. The earth belongs to them.

Here is one of their prayers, seasoned with a bit of irony:

Lord, keep me from becoming talkative and possessed with the idea that I must express myself on every subject.

Release me from the craving to straighten out everyone's affairs.

Teach me the glorious lesson that occasionally I may be wrong.

Make me helpful but not bossy.

With my vast store of wisdom and experience, it does seem a pity not to use it all—.
But thou knowest, Lord, that I want a few friends at the end. *Amen.*[9]

Jesus said, ". . . the meek . . . shall inherit the earth." Benito Mussolini and Adolf Hitler didn't believe that, for they attempted to take it by force. No one ever lived unhappier lives or died more despicable deaths than they.

How are we going to take care of this inner power urge, "the ego ambition?" Dr. Adler sought to appease this strong egotistical power urge so that it might work amicably with the widely different feelings of altruism that man also possesses.[10] To this end he urged his patients to follow the Golden Rule: "Thou shalt love thy neighbour as thyself."[11]

The weakness of the Adler plan was that he was looking only at the *power urge*, which is one symptom of our carnal nature, just as Freud centered his attention on another outstanding symptom—man's strong sexual and lustful propensity. The trouble with both Adler and Freud lies in treating merely *symptoms* of the carnal nature instead of directing therapy at the *cause*. When a person is dying of meningitis, it helps little to treat the symptom of headache with some aspirin and fail to attack the evil infection itself.

The Bible focuses therapy on the *cause* of the symptoms: the *carnal nature:* "And those who belong to Christ Jesus have crucified the lower nature with its passions and desires."[12]

Instead of making frequent, expensive and often futile trips to a psychiatrist's couch, we are invited by the Lord to make one trip to the cross for crucifixion of the trouble-maker. When we drive the spikes into everything in our lives that God has marked for destruction, then God, for Christ's sake, executes that old self which ever breathes out "ego ambition" and licentious, lustful living. "And, while Christ was actually taking upon Himself the sins of men, God condemned that sinful nature."[13]

"Wherefore Jesus also, that he might sanctify the people with his own blood, suffered without the gate. Let us go forth therefore unto him without the camp, bearing his reproach."[14] Now, if you go outside the gate, beyond the opinions and doctrines of man, for the crucifixion of that disease-maker, the old self, you will be able to say with Paul, "I am crucified with Christ; nevertheless I live; yet not I, but Christ liveth in me. . . ."[15]

CHAPTER 25

"Two Souls, Alas, Dwell in My Breast Apart"

ONE OF THE MOST BRUTAL MURDERS EVER COMMITTED happened on a summer evening some years ago. Joseph Ransler went to the home of his brother, who was working on a night shift. He visited with his brother's wife who, he later reported, "was dressed in shorts and a bra, like she always was." A few hours later Joseph made a sexual assault on the woman, and to cover up his crime he strangled her and her little daughter. The lifeless victims were found by Joseph's brother when he returned home from work.

After seven hours of questioning by the police, Joseph Ransler confessed and made this statement: "What makes a guy act like I do? I want to pray and everything, and inwardly I feel that I want to be the best Christian in the world. But outwardly I'm a maniac and I can't control the outward part. I don't know why." He hadn't made much headway following the inward voice, for the police had previously arrested him a half-dozen times.

However, his recognition of two forces working within him, one for the good and one for the bad, is worthy of notice. Sigmund Freud recognized the active conflict that occurs in a man's mind because of the presence of these two different forces. In fact, the Freudian school of psychoanalysis believes that this cerebral conflict is the source of most of man's psychic disorders.

In an earlier chapter we mentioned that Dr. Karl Menninger recognizes the existence of these two inner forces and refers to them as the "life instinct" and "death instinct." The life instinct of man seeks to preserve his life while the death instinct seeks to destroy it, as well as the lives of others. Dr. Menninger's book on suicide is aptly titled *Man Against Himself*.[1]

People standing near the brink of a deep canyon often sense an inner agent that wants to push them over the edge. But they also sense and usually heed another agent that causes them to step back.

Because the strong evil agent that dwells in man seeks his destruction, it is not surprising that in the United States there occur annually nineteen thousand suicides, not to mention the many who disguise their suicides successfully as an accident, and the many other thousands who attempt suicide but who fail in one way or another.

Carl Jung, the founder of the school of analytical psychology, was also impressed by the fact that neuroses were caused by the battle between two warring cerebral agents: "What drives people to war with themselves is the intuition or the knowledge that they consist of two persons in opposition to one another. The conflict may be between the sensual and the spiritual man. . . . It is what Faust means when he says, 'Two souls, alas, dwell in my breast.' . . . A neurosis is a dissociation of personality. Healing may be called a religious problem."[2]

Robert Louis Stevenson, in *Dr. Jekyl and Mr. Hyde*, gave a fascinating description of an individual who was swayed one moment by the beneficent Dr. Jekyl in his nature, and then the next minute he was turned into and controlled by his evil and murderous Mr. Hyde nature.

Modern psychologists and psychiatrists can give a clear-cut answer to the question of the sex murderer, Joseph Ransler, "What makes a guy act like I do?" Many other people sense their ambivalence—the presence of two inner forces, one good and one bad. Many individuals also recognize the greater power of the evil agent. Perhaps they haven't had to hang by the neck for their misdeeds, but many times they have had to hang their faces in shame.

With a little introspection, each of us can sense the presence of two opposite forces within; it is especially easy to sense our duality when we have a moral issue to decide. It is not pleasant to have two pugilists battling it out and making a rumpus in our cerebral attics.

Four thousand years before psychiatry awoke to the importance of two forces within man, God described this conflict in a drama recorded in the first book of the Bible.[3] To Abraham and his wife Sarah, God promised a son through whom all the nations of the earth would be blessed. With the passing of many years, Sarah became so old that she thought God had forgotten His promise. She decided to help out a dilatory Jehovah by lending her slave girl Hagar to Abraham so that he might obtain the promised heir whose posterity would bless all the nations of the world. Abraham consented to this human scheme without consulting God. In due time the slave girl bore Abraham a son and called him Ishmael.

Abraham was elated because he had a son and an heir. Now God could use Ishmael to fulfill the divine purpose. Holding Ishmael on his knee and tenderly caring for him from infancy, the aged patriarch felt strong affection for this one and only child. He beamed, doted, and wrapped his heart strings around Ishmael.

When Ishmael was thirteen years old, God shocked the blissful Abraham by telling him that Ishmael, born of the slave girl, was not the one through whom He would bless the world. God told Abraham that his shrunken, ninety-year-old wife Sarah was going to bear him a son through whom the promise would be fulfilled. The idea of setting aside Ishmael, the idol of his heart, greatly disturbed Abraham, who implored God, ". . . oh that Ishmael might live before thee!"[4]

God, knowing the nature of Ishmael and foreseeing the murderous tendencies in him and his posterity, could not grant Abraham's prayer. When Abraham recognized that God would not change, he accepted the divine plan. By faith a son was miraculously born to the aged Abraham and Sarah, and he was called Isaac.

As the years passed the conflict between these two basically different sons of Abraham and their two mothers became intense, bitter and murderous. Abraham's mind was in turmoil—as the mind of unregenerate man is upset by two warring elements under his cerebral roof. Abraham's mind would be pulled one moment by the appeals of the good son Isaac. Then his mind would be torn by the demands of Ishmael, who the angel predicted would be the son of lust and hate. Abraham was very conscious of these two diametrically opposed forces under his roof, just as Ransler the sex murderer sensed both the good and the bad forces within himself.

Because God saw that the hate in Ishmael's heart was

nearing the point of murder, He called Abraham to him
and told him to cast Ishmael out of his house. Cast out his
firstborn, his seventeen-year-old son, the idol of his heart?
Undoubtedly Abraham shed many a tear over this command,
but by faith he obeyed God. It was better to shed a
few tears over Ishmael's dismissal than to shed many more
over the murder of Isaac, the son through whom the Christ
was to come. One should remember that the tears Abraham
shed over Ishmael were the result of his getting outside
of God's will.

Paul tells us that these two sons of Abraham were symbolical
of the two natures within carnal man:

Now we, brethren, as Isaac was, are the children of promise.
But as then he that was born after the flesh persecuted
him that was born after the Spirit, even so it is now.
Nevertheless what saith the scripture? Cast out the bondwoman
and her son: for the son of the bondwoman shall
not be heir with the son of the freewoman. So then, brethren,
we are not children of the bondwoman, but of the
free.[5]

For the flesh lusteth against the Spirit, and the Spirit
against the flesh: and these are contrary the one to the
other: so that ye cannot do the things that ye would.[6]

In writing to the Romans, Paul describes two warring
forces within his own mind before he was filled with the
Holy Spirit. He dramatically describes the greater power
of the carnal force nineteen centuries before the birth of
psychiatry:

My own behavior baffles me. For I find myself not doing
what I really want to do but doing what I really loathe.
Yet surely if I do things I really don't want to do it cannot
be said that "I" am doing them at all—it must be sin that
has made its home in my nature. (And indeed, I know
from experience that the carnal side of my being can
scarcely be called the home of good!) I often find that I
have the will to do good, but not the power. That is, I
don't accomplish the good I set out to do, and the evil I
don't really want to do I find I am always doing. Yet if I
do things that I don't really want to do then it is not, I repeat,
"I" who do them, but the sin which has made its
home within me. When I come up against the Law [Mosaic
Law] I want to do good, but in practice I do evil. My conscious
mind whole-heartedly endorses the Law, yet I ob-

serve an entirely different principle at work in my nature. This is in continual conflict with my conscious attitude, and makes me an unwilling prisoner to the law of sin and death. In my mind I am God's willing servant, but in my own nature I am bound fast, as I say, to the law of sin and death. It is an agonising situation, and who on earth can set me free from the clutches of my own sinful nature?[7]

Here is the greatest human question of all time. Abraham, the Apostle Paul, and the sex murderer Ransler faced it. Everyone will have some important questions in the tomorrows, but none is as important as this one: ". . . Who on earth can set me free from the clutches of my own sinful nature?" If one fails here he will, in a sense, fail in every day that he lives.

There is no lack of answers. Every school of psychiatric thought has a different one—pretty good evidence that none is truly effective. Furthermore, these various schools concern themselves with merely treating symptoms. But there is a *cure* for mankind's agonizing situation.

CHAPTER 26

Freedom From
an Agonizing Situation

"WHO ON EARTH CAN SET ME FREE FROM THE CLUTCHES of my own sinful nature?" This question asked long ago by the Apostle Paul is being asked by millions of people today. It was the question that troubled two psychiatrists— husband and wife—as they held a consultation in their offices in Chicago. They were discussing the best way to free a patient from a serious situation.

Dr. Lena Sadler had asked her husband, Dr. William S. Sadler, to see one of her patients, a "refined, highly educated" woman. The patient still did not respond, even after their combined psychiatric counselings. Dr. William Sadler advised his wife that she need not expect any worthwhile improvement "until her patient's mental life was set in order and numerous psychic slivers were removed." To the question of how long did he think that would take, he replied, "Probably a year or more."

Now let Dr. William Sadler tell in his own words what happened:

Imagine my surprise when this patient walked into my office a few days later and informed me that her "troubles were over," that the things she had assured me a few days previously she "could never do," had all been done, that everything I had asked her to do as part of her "cure" had been set in operation—she had completely overhauled her social, family, and personal life, had made numerous "confessions," and had accomplished a score of almost impossible mental and "moral" stunts.

In reply to my astonished question, "How in the world did you ever do all this and effect this great change in your mental attitude toward yourself and the world in less than one week?" she smilingly replied, "Dr. Lena taught me to pray."[1]

Without further long, drawn-out and expensive sessions in a psychiatrist's office, the woman had confessed her sins to God and to others. Then she experienced *immediately* the healing and refreshment of the promise of Jesus: "Peace I leave with you, my peace I give unto you: not as the world giveth, give I unto you. Let not your heart be troubled, neither let it be afraid."[2]

Dr. Carl Jung also recognized the importance of God in healing the ills of mankind:

I should like to call attention to the following facts. During the past thirty years, people from all the civilized countries of the earth have consulted me. I have treated many hundreds of patients. . . . Among all my patients in the second half of life—that is to say, over thirty-five—there has not been *one* whose problem in the last resort was not that of finding a religious outlook on life. . . .

It seems to me, that, side by side with the decline of religious life, the neuroses grow noticeably more frequent. . . .

The patient is looking for something that will take possession of him and give meaning and form to the confusion of his neurotic mind. Is the doctor equal to the task? To begin with, he will probably hand over his patient to the clergyman or the philosopher, or abandon him to that perplexity which is the special note of our day.... Human thought cannot conceive any system or final truth that could give the patient what he needs in order to live: that is faith, hope, love, and insight....

There are however persons who, while well aware of the psychic nature of their complaint, nevertheless refuse to turn to the clergyman. They do not believe that he can really help them. Such persons distrust the doctor for the same reason, and they are justified by the fact that both doctor and clergyman *stand before them with empty hands, if not—what is even worse—with empty words*.... It is from the clergyman, not from the doctor, that the sufferers should expect such help.[8]

Freud, Adler, and Jung largely agreed that many of man's mental disturbances are due to *conflict* between inner good and evil forces. Freud emphasized the *sexual propensities* of the bad force, Adler stressed the *ruthless drive* of the carnal nature for power and supremacy, while Jung likened the evil part of man to a *wild, ravenous wolf*.

In the 1930's, specialists in psychosomatic medicine began to learn that a host of *physical diseases* were caused by envy, jealousy, self-centeredness, resentment, fear and hatred—*the identical emotions that the Bible lists as attributes of our wolfish nature. Hence, we see that most of the mental and physical ills of man are caused by the activities of an inner evil force.* Understandable is the inefficacy of human agents to free man from an innate evil nature that is tied as tightly to him as a corpse was bound to a condemned criminal in ancient times.

Paul himself answered the question he had raised:

I thank God there *is* a way out through Jesus Christ our Lord.[4]

... *while Christ was actually taking upon Himself the sins of men, God condemned that sinful nature.* So that ... we are living no longer by the dictates of our sinful nature, but in obedience to the promptings of the Spirit.[5]

Now if Christ does live within you His presence means that your sinful nature is dead....[6]

By His death and resurrection Jesus did not automatically deliver every man from the bondage of his lower nature. He made this freedom available through our obedience to these divine conditions:

. . . if . . . you cut the nerve of your instinctive actions by obeying the Spirit, you are on the way to real living.[7]

So that . . . we are living no longer by the dictates of our sinful nature, but in obedience to the promptings of the Spirit.[8]

And those who belong to Christ Jesus have crucified the lower nature with its passions and desires.[9]

Then put to death those parts of you which belong to the earth— fornication, indecency, lust, foul cravings, and the ruthless greed which is nothing less than idolatry.[10]

But now you yourselves must lay aside all anger, passion, malice, cursing, filthy talk—have done with them! Stop lying to one another, now that you have discarded the old nature with its deeds and have put on the new nature, which is being constantly renewed in the image of its Creator and brought to know God.[11]

Billy Graham expresses well the part we must play: "It is only when we come to the *will* that we find the very heart of repentance. There must be that determination to forsake sin—to change one's attitude toward self, toward sin, and God; to change one's feeling: to change one's will, disposition, and purpose. . . . There is not one verse of Scripture that indicates you can be a Christian and live any kind of a life you want to."[12]

Paul tells us that Abraham, with two warring sons under his roof, was a symbol of the two forces within man's mind.[13] But Paul makes the application for us: "Nevertheless what saith the scripture? Cast out the . . . son. . . ." [14] It will give us pain to bid a final farewell to the carnal part of our natures which has given us a large share of life's so-called pleasures. It will mean giving up some of our habits, our friends, our practices, and our ways of thinking. Let us face it squarely—it is a sorrowful experience to bid adieu to every worldly pleasure, friend and habit that God marks for dismissal. Yet it is not a dismissal of worthwhile joys and friends but of those born, like Ishmael, outside of God's will for our lives.

" 'I promise you,' " returned Jesus, 'nobody leaves home or brothers or sisters or mother or father or children or property for my sake or the Gospel's without getting back a hundred times over, now in this present life; . . . and in the next world eternal life.' "[15]

Jesus recognizes that we feel some pain in giving up that which is carnal, but He promises that we will receive here and now one hundred times as much of the worthwhile. His statement is understandable when we realize the vast array of mental and physical diseases from which we are freed when we, with God's help, cast out the innate troublemaker.

We may shed some tears in saying farewell to the old life and its lure, but our grief will seem inconsequential moments later when we experience the exhilaration of His resurrection, life, and power within us: "For if we have grown jointly with Him in experiencing a similar death, then the same must be true of our resurrection with Him, aware of this, that our old self has been jointly crucified with Him, so that the sin-controlled body might be devitalized and we no longer be slaves of sin.[16]

Surrendering one's will to the divine will may seem to be a negative procedure, but it gives positive dividends. Psychologist Wallace Emerson writes, "It is a will that, while giving up the mastery, has finally become something of a master in its own house. . . ."[17] Only when we do our part in crucifying the inner troublemaker, and in opening the door so that Christ may occupy the throne room of the soul, can we experience real living, new strength and vitality, life and inward peace, and the fullness of the promise, ". . . none of these diseases. . . ."

CHAPTER 1
1. S. E. Massengill, *A Sketch of Medicine and Pharmacy* (Bristol, Tenn., S. E. Massengill Company, 1943), p. 16.
2. *Ibid.*
3. *Scope* (Summer 1955), p. 13.
4. Massengill, *op. cit.*, pp. 16-17.
5. Acts 7:22, KJV.
6. Exodus 15:26, KJV.
7. George Rosen, *History of Public Health* (New York, MD Publications, 1958), pp. 62-63.
8. Fielding Garrison, *History of Medicine* (Philadelphia, W. B. Saunders Co., 1929), p. 187.
9. Rosen, *op. cit.*, pp. 63-65.
10. Arturo Castiglione, *A History of Medicine* (New York, Alfred A. Knopf, Inc., 1941), p. 71.

CHAPTER 2
1. Deuteronomy 23:12-13, BERKELEY.
2. Arturo Castiglione, *op. cit.*, p. 70.
3. Numbers 19, KJV.
4. *An Epitome of the History of Medicine,* second edition (Philadelphia, F. A. Davis Co., 1901), p. 326.

CHAPTER 3
1. Harold Thomas Hyman, *An Integrated Practice of Medicine* (Philadelphia, W. B. Saunders Co., 1946), p. 2551.
2. Hiram N. Wineberg, "The Rare Occurrence of Cancer of the Womb Among Jewish Women," *Bulletin of Mt. Sinai Hospital* (1919).
3. I. Kaplan, and R. Rosh, *American Journal of Roentgenology* (June 1947), pp. 659-664.
4. "Cancer of Cervix and Non-Jews," *Journal of the American Medical Association* (July 23, 1949), p. 1069.
5. W. B. Ober, and L. Reiner, "Cancer of Cervix in Jewish Women," *New England Journal of Medicine* (November 30, 1954), pp. 555-559.

6. A. Symeonidis, "Acta Union Internationale Contre le Cancer," *Bulletin of U. S. Public Health Service* (Vol. VII, No. 1), p. 127; P. S. Rao, R. S. Reddy, and D. J. Reddy, "A Study of the Etiological Factors in Guntur," *Journal of the American Medical Association* (November 7, 1959), p. 1421.

7. S. L. Israel, "Relative Infrequency of Cervical Carcinoma in Jewish Women: Is the Enigma Solved?" *American Journal of Obstetrics and Gynecology* (March 1955), pp. 358-360.

8. A. J. Paquin, Jr., and J. M. Pearce, *Journal of Urology* (November 1955), pp. 626-627.

9. Genesis 17:10-12.

10. Martin C. Rosenthal, *Journal of the American Medical Association* (February 1947), p. 436.

11. L. Emmett Holt, Jr., and Rustin McIntosh, *Holt Pediatrics*, twelfth edition (New York, Appleton-Century-Crofts, Inc., 1953), pp. 125-126.

12. Genesis 17:12, KJV.

13. Colossians 2:11, NEB.

14. Colossians 3:5-9, NEB.

15. J. D. Ratcliff, "Stress the Cause of All Disease?" *Reader's Digest* (January 1955), pp. 24-28.

16. Deuteronomy 10:12, 16; Jeremiah 4:4; Romans 2:28-29; 4:11; Galatians 6:13-15.

17. Acts 15:22-30.

18. Galatians 5:24, NEB.

CHAPTER 4

1. Milton Golin, "Robber of Five Million Brains," *Journal of the American Medical Association* (July 19, 1958), p. 1496.

2. "Motor-Vehicle Accidents," *Journal of the American Medical Association* (March 30, 1957), p. 1149.

3. *New York State Department of Health Bulletin,* (Vol. XIV, May 29, 1961), p. 85.

4. *Ibid.* (Vol. XI, July 14, 1958), p. 113.

5. William N. Plymat, *Buffalo Evening News* (July 29, 1960), p. 1.

6. "Incidence of Violent Deaths Tied to Alcohol Reported High," *Medical Tribune* (July 25, 1960), p. 4.

7. Eli Robins, "Recognition and Management of the Seriously Suicidal Patient," *Medical Science* (July 25, 1960), p. 78.

8. Russell L. Cecil and Robert F. Loeb, *Textbook of Medicine* (Philadelphia, W. B. Saunders Co., 1959), p. 1653.

9. *Ibid.*

10. Frederick Lemere, "Final Outcome of Alcoholism," *Modern Medicine* (July 15, 1953), p. 110.
11. *Othello,* ii. 3. 293.
12. Psalm 84:11, KJV.
13. "A Problem in Business and Industry," *Yale Center of Alcohol Studies,* p. 251.
14. "Alcoholism," *Journalism of the American Medical Association* (August 7, 1954), p. 1366.
15. *Ibid.*
16. Howard Earle, "They're Helping the Alcoholic Worker," *Today's Health* (December 1960), p. 73.
17. Proverbs 23:19-21, 29-34, MOFFATT.

CHAPTER 5
1. Alton Ochsner, *Smoking and Cancer* (New York, Julian Messner, Inc., 1954), p. 12.
2. *Today's Health* (March 1959), p. 54.
3. Victor H. Handy, "Lung Cancer in Men," *Health News* (November 1958), p. 16.
4. Ochsner, *op. cit.,* p. 18.
5. *Ibid.,* p. 4.
6. *Ibid.,* p. 14.
7. David Rutstein, *Cancer* (March-April 1958), p. 46.
8. E. C. Hammond and Daniel Horn, "Smoking and Death Rates—Report on 44 Months of Follow-Up of 187,783 Men," *Journal of the American Medical Association* (March 15, 1958), pp. 1294-1308.
9. *Ibid.,* p. 1308.
10. *Scope* (February 13, 1957).
11. L. E. Burney, "Smoking and Lung Cancer," *Journal of the American Medical Association* (November 28, 1959), p. 1829; L. M. Miller, and James Monahan, "The Facts Behind Filter-Tip Cigarettes," *Reader's Digest* (July 1957), pp. 33-39.
12. "Mortality From Selected Causes, by Age, Race, and Sex: United States, 1959," *Vital Statistics* (September 22, 1961).
13. E. C. Hammond, and Daniel Horn, *op. cit.,* p. 1307.
14. *Ibid.,* p. 1305.
15. *World Almanac and Book of Facts for 1960* (New York, *New York World Telegram and the Sun),* p. 307.
16. H. S. Hedges, "Eye Damage By Alcohol," *Journal of the American Medical Association* (February 18, 1956), p. 604.
17. J. D. Spillane, "Nicotine and the Nervous System," *Journal of the American Medical Association* (February 18, 1956), p. 584.

18. "Cigarette Smoking," *Journal of the American Medical Association* (May 19, 1956), p. 301.

19. E. C. Hammond, and Daniel Horn, *op. cit.*, p. 1296.

20. Francis C. Lowell, William Franklin, Alan L. Michelson, and Irving W. Schiller, *The New England Journal of Medicine* (January 19, 1956).

21. "Smoking and Asthma," *Journal of the American Medical Association* (December 12, 1952), p. 1540.

22. F. L. Rosen, and A. Levy, "Bronchial Asthma Due to Allergy to Tobacco Smoke in an Infant," *Journal of the American Medical Association* (October 21, 1950), pp. 620-621.

23. E. C. Hammond, and Daniel Horn, *op. cit.*, p. 1306.

24. *Ibid.*

25. P. Bernhard, "Injurious Effects of Cigarette Smoking in Women," *Journal of the American Medical Association* (October 15, 1949), p. 492.

26. I Corinthians 6:19-20, KJV.

27. I Corinthians 3:17, KJV.

28. I Corinthians 10:31, KJV.

CHAPTER 6

1. Harold Thomas Hyman, *An Integrated Practice of Medicine* (Philadelphia, W. B. Saunders Co., 1946), p. 332.

2. Exodus 34:7, KJV.

3. I Corinthians 10:8, ASV.

4. Johan Wintzell, *Svenska lakartidningen* (April 2, 1954), abstracted in the *Journal of the American Medical Association* (July 15, 1954), p. 1097.

5. I Corinthians 6:18, ASV.

6. Ernst Epstein, "Failure of Penicillin in Treatment of Acute Gonorrhea in American Troops in Korea," *Journal of the American Medical Association* (March 7, 1959), p. 1054.

7. *Journal of the American Medical Association* (February 13, 1954), p. 608.

8. "Syphilis Again on the Increase," *Journal of the American Medical Association* (April 20, 1957), p. 1545.

9. Howard Whitman, "The Slavery of Sex Freedom," *Better Homes & Gardens* (June 1957), p. 59.

10. Sylvanus M. Duvall, "Fiction and Facts About Sex," *Reader's Digest* (June 1960), p. 128.

11. Walter Lentino, "Evaluation of a System of Legalized Prostitution," *Journal of the American Medical Association* (May 7, 1955), p. 22.

12. Harold Thomas Hyman, *op. cit.*, p. 1465.

13. Proverbs 5:1-12, MOFFATT.
14. I Thessalonians 4:3-8, PHILLIPS.
15. Harold Thomas Hyman, *op. cit.*, p. 332.
16. R. H. Kampmeier, "Management of Syphilis," *Modern Medicine* (July 15, 1953), p. 88.
17. Mark 10:4-9, KJV.

CHAPTER 7
1. Alfred C. Kinsey, Wardell B. Pomeroy, Clyde E. Martin and Paul H. Gebhard, *Sexual Behavior in the Human Female* (Philadelphia, W. B. Saunders Co., 1953).
2. Romans 1:24-32; Mark 7:20-23; Galatians 5:19-21, KJV.
3. Edmund Bergler, and William S. Kroger, "Sexual Behavior," *Journal of the American Medical Association* (January 9, 1954), p. 168.
4. Alfred C. Kinsey, et al, *op. cit.*, p. 327.
5. William J. Brown, "Current Status of Syphilis in the United States," *Erie County Bulletin* (February 1961), p. 10.
6. Alfred C. Kinsey, et al, *op. cit.*, pp. 328-330, 385-390,
7. Edmund Bergler, and William S. Kroger, *op. cit.*, p. 168.
8. Review of *Kinsey's Myth of Female Sexuality: The Medical Facts* (Edmund Bergler and William S. Kroger), in the *Journal of the American Medical Association* (April 17, 1954), p. 1396.
9. Irving J. Sands, "Marriage Counseling as a Medical Responsibility," *New York State Journal of Medicine* (July 15, 1954), p. 2052.
10. Maurice Zolotow, "Love Is Not a Statistic," *Reader's Digest* (April 1954), p. 9.
11. *Ibid.*
12. Howard Whitman, "The Slavery of Sex Freedom," *Better Homes & Gardens* (June 1957), p. 219.
13. Hebrews 13:4, KJV.
14. "Youth and the Natural Urge," *Better Homes & Gardens* (July 1957), p. 43.
15. Mark 10:6-8, ASV.
16. Irving J. Sands, *op. cit.*, pp. 2052-2055.

CHAPTER 8
1. Carl Jung, *Modern Man in Search of a Soul* (New York, Harcourt, Brace and Co., Inc., 1933), p. 260.
2. I Corinthians 13:4-5, 7-8, NEB.
3. New York, Simon and Schuster, Inc., 1956, pp. 3-15.

4. *Psychoanalysis and Religion* (New Haven, Yale University Press, 1950), pp. 86-87.
5. "Sex in Modern Life," *Current Medical Digest* (September 1961), p. 55.
6. I Corinthians 13:11, 13, NEB.
7. Luke 15:11-32.
8. Paul H. Landis, "Don't Expect Too Much of Sex in Marriage," *Reader's Digest* (December 1954), pp. 26-27.
9. I Corinthians 10:13, KJV.

CHAPTER 9
1. *Journal of the American Medical Association* (May 29, 1948), p. 442.
2. J. D. Ratcliff, *Reader's Digest* (January 1955), pp. 24-28.
3. *Personality Manifestations in Psychosomatic Illness* (Philadelphia, Edward Stern & Co., 1953).
4. *Scope* (November 13, 1947).

CHAPTER 10
1. Galatians 5:19-21, PHILLIPS.
2. Galatians 5:24, MOFFATT.
3. *Practice of Psychiatry* (St. Louis, C. V. Mosby Co., 1953), p. 1008.
4. *Macbeth*, v. 3. 38.
5. *Ibid,*, v. 3. 40.
6. *The Way to Security* (Garden City, N. Y., Doubleday & Co., Inc., 1951), p. 52.
7. Hebrews 12:14-15, PHILLIPS.
8. Galatians 5:24, PHILLIPS.

CHAPTER 11
1. Dale Carnegie, *How to Stop Worrying and Start Living* (New York, Simon and Schuster, Inc., 1948), p. 101.
2. William J. Grace, and Harold G. Wolff, "Treatment of Ulcerative Colitis," *Journal of the American Medical Association* (July 14, 1951), p. 981.
3. George W. Gray, "Anxiety and Illness," *Harper's* (May 1939), p. 610.
4. Dale Carnegie, *op. cit.*, p. 101.
5. Proverbs 15:17, MOFFATT.
6. Luke 9:55, KJV.
7. Acts 7:60, KJV.
8. Colossians 3:5, 7-10, 13-14, MOFFATT.

CHAPTER 12
1. Matthew 5:41, ASV.
2. Matthew 5:40 ASV.

CHAPTER 13
1. I Corinthians 13:4-5, ASV.
2. *What Life Should Mean to You* (Boston, Little, Brown and Co., 1931), p. 258.
3. Matthew 22:37-40, ASV.
4. Matthew 5:44, KJV.
5. Edwin Markham, "Outwitted," *Poems of Edwin Markham* (New York, Harper & Brothers, 1950), p. 18. Reprinted by permission of Virgil Markham.

CHAPTER 14
1. *Health News* (February 1955), p. 9.
2. I Thessalonians 5:18, PHILLIPS.
3. Philippians 4:6-7, PHILLIPS.
4. Philippians 4:8, KJV.

CHAPTER 15
1. Paul B. Roen, "Atherosclerosis," *General Practice* (January 1959), p. 11.
2. Leviticus 7:22-24, KJV.
3. Leviticus 3:17.
4. Russell L. Cecil, and Robert F. Loeb, *A Textbook of Medicine* (Philadelphia, W. B. Saunders Co., 1959), p. 645.
5. Titus 1:12-13, BERKELEY.
6. E. C. Hammond, and Daniel Horn, "Smoking and Death Rates," *Journal of the American Medical Association* (March 15, 1958), p. 1304.
7. "Vital Statistics," *National Summaries* (April 24, 1959), p. 130.
8. "Free-Fatty-Acid Rise Tied to Smoking," *Medical News* (June 2, 1961), p. 1.
9. Harold Gretzinger, "No Time to Waste," *Christian Life* (February, 1949).
10. Psalm 91:3-7, KJV.
11. Psalm 46:1-3, KJV.
12. Psalm 46:10-11, ASV.

CHAPTER 16
1. Psalm 27:1-3, BERKELEY.
2. Harold Thomas Hyman, *An Integrated Practice of Medicine* (Philadelphia, W. B. Saunders Co., 1946), p. 909.
3. Psalm 56:3-4, BERKELEY.
4. W. T. Purkiser, *Exploring the Old Testament* (Kansas City, Beacon Hill Press, 1960), p. 25.
5. Psalm 23:1-4, KJV.

CHAPTER 17
1. Matthew 5:40, KJV.

2. "Influence of Some Drugs and Emotions on Blood Coagulation," *Journal of the American Medical Association* (January 26, 1952), p. 269.
3. R. H. Rosenman, and M. Friedman, "Stress Affects Serum Cholesterol and Clotting Time," *Medical Newsletter* (November—December, 1957), p. 1; Stewart Wolf, "Emotional Tension Alone Is Found to Raise Serum Cholesterol Level," *Scope* (January 6, 1960), p. 1; "Stress and Heart Disease," *Modern Concepts of Cardiovascular Disease* (American Heart Association, July 1960), p. 599.
4. Psalm 34:4, KJV.

CHAPTER 18
1. Dale Carnegie, *op. cit.*, pp. 253-254.
2. Isaiah 26:3, KJV.
3. *Practice of Psychiatry* (St. Louis, C. V. Mosby Co., 1953), pp. 1012-1013.
4. Psalm 103:12, KJV.
5. I John 4:18, KJV.
6. Proverbs 16:7, KJV.
7. I Corinthians 15:54-55, KJV.
8. "Thanatopsis."

CHAPTER 19
1. John 11:25-26, BERKELEY.
2. Luke 8:52, ASV.
3. I Thessalonians 4:13, BERKELEY.
4. I Corinthians 15:21, BERKELEY.
5. I Corinthians 15:22, KJV.
6. II Corinthians 4:17-18, BERKELEY.
7. Philippians 4:6-7, BERKELEY.

CHAPTER 20
1. Frederick Langbridge, "A Cluster of Quiet Thoughts" (published by the Religious Tract Society).
2. *The Stress of Life* (New York, McGraw-Hill Book Co., Inc., 1956), p. 154.
3. II Corinthians 12:8-10, BERKELEY.
4. Mark 6:31, KJV.
5. "A Scientific Report on What Hope Does for Man" (New York State Heart Assembly, 105 East 22nd Street, New York, New York).
6. John Bunyan, *Grace Abounding to the Chief of Sinners* (Philadelphia, J. J. Woodward, 1928), p. 148.
7. Genesis 37:35, BERKELEY.
8. Genesis 42:36, KJV.
9. Genesis 47:9, BERKELEY.
10. II Corinthians 11:24-27, BERKELEY.

11. Romans 8:35-37, PHILLIPS.
12. Romans 8:37, KJV.

CHAPTER 21
1. Philadelphia, W. B. Saunders Co., 1959, p. 1653.
2. William Wordsworth, "My Heart Leaps Up."
3. Psalm 34:11-14, MOFFATT.

CHAPTER 22
1. *Psychiatry in General Practice* (Philadelphia, W. B. Saunders Co., 1949), pp. 265-268.
2. S. Arieti, *Interpretation of Schizophrenia* (New York, Robert Brunner, 1955), p. 3.
3. *Practice of Psychiatry* (St. Louis, C. V. Mosby Co., 1953), p. 396.
4. Proverbs 22:15, ASV.
5. Exodus 20:9, ASV.
6. II Thessalonians 3:10, KJV.
7. "Psychiatry At Work," *Time* (July 18, 1955), p. 55.
8. Philippians 4:7, KJV.
9. John 14:27, ASV.
10. *The Merck Manual* (Rahway, N. J., Merck & Co., 1956), p. 1311.
11. Philippians 2:4, PHILLIPS.
12. Ephesians 4:31-32, PHILLIPS.
13. Romans 12:10, PHILLIPS.
14. Romans 14:19, PHILLIPS.
15. Mark 6:31, ASV.

CHAPTER 23
1. Luke 6:38, ASV.
2. Smiley Blanton, *Love or Perish* (New York, Simon and Schuster, Inc., 1956), p. 4.
3. Harry J. Johnson, *Blue Print for Health* (Chicago, Blue Cross Association, Summer 1962), p. 19.
4. John D. Rockefeller, Sr., *Outlook* (October 7, 1905), pp. 300-301.
5. I John 3:14, BERKELEY.
6. Romans 12:16, BERKELEY.
7. Romans 12:16, PHILLIPS.
8. Matthew 16:25, KJV.

CHAPTER 24
1. *Understanding Human Nature* (Garden City, N. Y., Garden City Publishing Co., 1927), pp. 285-286; *Individual Psychology and Social Problems* (London, The C. S. Daniel Co., 1932), pp. 15, 22.
2. Romans 12:3, PHILLIPS.
3. Romans 12:9-10, 16, BERKELEY.
4. James 3:1, PHILLIPS.

5. Philippians 2:2-3, PHILLIPS.
6. Matthew 23:5-12, PHILLIPS.
7. Psalm 119:165, KJV.
8. Matthew 5:5, KJV.
9. Anonymous.
10. *What Life Should Mean to You* (Boston, Little, Brown and Co., 1931), p. 258.
11. Matthew 19:19, KJV.
12. Galatians 5:24, NEB.
13. Romans 8:3, PHILLIPS.
14. Hebrews 13:12-13, KJV.

CHAPTER 25
1. New York, Harcourt, Brace and Co., Inc., 1938, p. 81.
2. *Modern Man in Search of a Soul* (New York, Harcourt, Brace and Co., Inc., 1933), p. 273.
3. Genesis 21, KJV.
4. Genesis 17:18, ASV.
5. Galatians 4:28-31, KJV.
6. Galatians 5:17, KJV.
7. Romans 7:15-24, PHILLIPS.

CHAPTER 26
1. *Theory and Practice of Psychiatry* (St. Louis, C. V. Mosby Co., 1936), p. 1075.
2. John 14:27, KJV.
3. Carl G. Jung, *Modern Man in Search of a Soul* (New York, Harcourt, Brace and Co., Inc., 1933), pp. 260-262.
4. Romans 7:25, PHILLIPS.
5. Romans 8:3-4, PHILLIPS.
6. Romans 8:10, PHILLIPS.
7. Romans 8:13, PHILLIPS.
8. Romans 8:4, PHILLIPS.
9. Galatians 5:24, NEB.
10. Colossians 3:5, NEB.
11. Colossians 3:8-10, NEB.
12. *Peace With God* (New York, Permabooks, 1955), pp. 124-125.
13. Galatians 4:28-31; 5:17, KJV.
14. Galatians 4:30, KJV.
15. Mark 10:30-31, PHILLIPS.
16. Romans 6:5-6, BERKELEY.
17. *Outline of Psychology* (Wheaton, Ill., Van Kampen Press), p. 453.